As a friend and fellow minister I respect g
minded commitment to Gospel ministry w
a meticulous analysis of some key expres
that will provide a valuable contribution to the development of effective
practice for years to come.

Rev Elfed Godding, National Director of Evangelical Alliance Wales

David Ollerton brings a rare combination to the table – a deep
understanding of the spiritual heritage of Wales, a love and concern for
the contemporary church, plus vision and faith for the future. Anyone
wanting to be a part of what the Lord will be accomplishing in Wales in
the coming years needs to read this significant and strategic book.

Nigel James, Elim in Wales

This book is like a piece of quality Welsh coal. It's been mined from
deep within this land with meticulous care and considerable effort. I am
convinced that, in the hands of diligent readers with an openness to the
Spirit of God, there is enough fuel here to help relight fires in the many
villages, towns and cities across our nation that long since have died down
or been extinguished.

Paul Smethurst, Minister of the Baptist Union of Wales

A *New Mission to Wales* is not only the fruit of successful doctoral thesis, but also the fruit of an individual's commitment to the work of the Gospel in Wales for over 20 years. Although David Ollerton is a Lancastrian by birth, the Lord has not only given him a burden for Wales, but a perception and discernment to recognise the present patterns, as well as the future needs, in order to ensure a thriving witness in our future. This volume, along with his work with Waleswide, sets a clear direction for those whose heart is to see growing and relevant churches throughout our country.

Meirion Morris, General Secretary of The Presbyterian Church of Wales

Have you ever asked yourself the question:
- what approaches to mission does God appear to be using across Wales?
- why are some churches growing and others not?
- to what extent is my church's approach to mission right?
- in what ways does our church need to change in order to reach our community?
- what should we do?

In short, do you long to reach your community in Wales effectively? If so, this book will be an extremely valuable tool. Based on sound research it will stimulate and encourage your thinking. It will lift your heart and keep your feet on the ground. It flows from a burdened heart and is driven by a burning desire to encourage and help church leaders.

David Norbury, former General Secretary of the Evangelical Movement of Wales, Executive Committee member of United Beach Missions

A New Mission to Wales

Seeing churches prosper across Wales
in the twenty-first century

David Ollerton
Waleswide / Cymrugyfan

CYHOEDDIADAU'R
GAIR

Waleswide is a collaboration of evangelical churches and organisations for the planting and strengthening of churches across Wales. It sees the need for an intentional and collaborative approach to church planting and strengthening in Wales. Waleswide works with leaders to see churches established especially where there is no evangelical church presence, and where churches need to be strengthened in their effectiveness.

For further information see www.waleswide.org.

Published by:
Cyhoeddiadau'r Gair
Ael y Bryn, Chwilog,
Pwllheli, Gwynedd
LL53 6SH.
www.ysgolsul.com

Contents

Introduction

Mission used to be seen as something going on overseas, which churches supported. We assumed that ours was a Christian land, and Wales a Christian country. No longer. In the twenty-first century, Wales is in a changed world of post-Christendom, secularism and materialism, and is largely post-Christian. The Christian identity that remains is nominal, and vibrant Christian presence, in many communities, is difficult to find. Wales is a mission-field once again.

Not all of the UK is quite like this. Churches are being planted, renewed and growing. Why is this not the case here? Some are growing, but too often by attracting existing Christians with what they offer. In many areas, people coming to faith in Christ from outside the church is a rarity. More people are going to heaven than coming to church for the first time, and grey hair is on the increase!

Why is this? Why do approaches to mission and evangelism, that are said to be successful elsewhere, not work as well here? What is different about Wales? What is it about our context that needs a 'Made in Wales' approach, and what is that approach? Jesus will build his Church, but we need to be wise co-workers with Him.

This book looks, first, at the distinctive *Aspects* of Wales [Part One]. It then looks at how we have been doing mission, and how appropriate different *Approaches* have been in the context of Wales [Part Two]. We can then look at best practice, and draw some lessons for the future [Part Three]. The interplay between the six *Aspects* of Welsh contexts, and the six *Approaches* to mission is the basis of the book.

In reading the book, the temptation will be to skim through the *Aspects* of Wales [Section One] and how the different *Approaches* got on [Section Two], to get to the application quickly [Section Three]. Your call ... but the outworkings will make more sense if we fully understand the *Aspects* and *Approaches*. You may want to go 'back and fore' to get the clearest grasp. Either way, the purpose of the book is to help us all to understand our particular context better, and so be more effective ... and perhaps more missional to areas outside our immediate patch.

The book has grown out of *Waleswide's* research over the past five years. Hundreds of leaders from all networks and denominations filled in the Questionnaire of 2012. This was followed by more than eighty follow-up interviews in 2013 and 2014, and then by sixteen regional 'Soundings' in which leaders gathered to consider the present and the needs of the future.

The research focussed on Nonconformist churches, traditional and modern, but the findings will be applicable, to some extent, to all denominations. The non-inclusion of Anglican churches was not from a sectarian motive, but for two practical reasons. Firstly, a version of the Questionnaire was sent to many Anglican leaders, but only a handful responded. *Waleswide* was not sufficiently well known, despite continual efforts. Secondly, the scale of the work was getting beyond what could be handled effectively, so it was decided not to try again to extend the scope of the research.

The research was done originally as a thesis for Chester University, so that its findings were subject to thorough rigour and evaluation. We have tried to be as thorough as possible, in order to be as relevant as possible. The original thesis had over 2,000 footnote references, and over 600 books, articles and sources, to support statements and to point to further reading. Most of these have not been included here in order to simplify things. They can be viewed in the full version, on application via the *Waleswide* website.

Just a few words of thanks:

- To the hundreds of leaders in Wales, for completing the questionnaire and giving time for the interviews and *Soundings*. Without you there would be no book.

- To the *Waleswide* team, and especially to David Dry for hours and hours of support, counsel and help.

- To Keith Warrington for your relentless encouragement, and to Dewi Hughes for your clarity.

- As ever, to Liz for your love and patience.

David Ollerton
Spring 2016

Section One:

Aspects: **Why and how is Wales different?**

Wales is distinguished from the other nations of the United Kingdom through political devolution, spoken language and accents, loyalties on the sports field, and by a boundary line on the map. In terms of mission, however, these features could be merely superficial, and not relevant to mission. This section will explore the apparent characteristics of Welsh people, society, history, culture and place that do demonstrate distinctive Welsh elements of context that cannot be ignored.

Adjusting our mission to our particular context is vital:

"The Christian Gospel is incarnational or it is nothing. There is no gospel that does not manifest itself in a specific context, in a time and in a place. The divine does not by-pass the flesh therefore questions of history, culture and identity are inevitable and theologically valid".[1]

---

1 D. Morgan, *Wales and the Word: Historical Perspectives on Religion and Welsh Identity* (Cardiff: University of Wales Press, 2008), 120.

However, the nature of Welsh contexts is a complex matter that needs to be unravelled.[2] Wales, according to Rees is, "a broth ... thousands of years in the brewing".[3] The context of Wales is not static, but evolving, changing and varied. For those looking at Wales from the outside a stereotypical caricature may be formed of sheep, rugby posts, pit winding gear, and ladies wearing tall black hats. Such images are indicators of a declining or, in some cases, an extinct tradition. As such, they may generate a mythology that appeals to tourists, but have little to do with reality.

The elements that do mark a difference are the everyday things of Welsh sport, music, language, attitudes, cultural events and media. Williams described these as "symbolic border guards" that identify people as belonging, or not, to Wales.[4] They help to distinguish Wales from the "other", the non-Welsh, particularly the English.[5] A notorious entry in the index of the 1880 edition of the Encyclopaedia Britannica had directed it's readers, "For Wales see England".[6] This reflected an official government policy to subsume Wales as an English region, referred to in the Act of Union of 1535 as the "Dominion of Wales".[7] Creating markers to defend a distinct identity, especially from England and Englishness, is no small part of Welsh identity and context.

These markers suggest differences, and yet do not produce a prototype

---

2 G. Day, *Making Sense of Wales, A Sociological Perspective* (Cardiff: University of Wales Press, 2002), 27.

3 J. Rees, *Bred of Heaven* (London: Profile, 2011), 8.

4 C. Williams, "Passports to Wales? Race, Nation and Identity," in *Nation, Identity and Social Theory: Perspectives from Wales* (ed. R. Fevre and A. Thompson; Cardiff: University of Wales Press, 1999), 82.

5 G. A. Williams, *When was Wales?* (Harmondsworth: Penguin, 1985), 304.

6 H. Carter, *Against the Odds: The Survival of Welsh Identity* (Cardiff: Institute of Welsh Affairs, 2010), 50.

7 A. Elias, "Political Representation," in *Understanding Contemporary Wales* (ed. H. Mackay; Cardiff: University of Wales Press, 2010), 233.

Welshman. There are differences in the regions of Wales that are more significant than the few features that can be said to be held in common. Wales is divided between north and south, urban and rural, by language, culture and by degrees of Britishness. These differences can bring discord more than unity, and things held dear in one region can exclude and alienate people in another. Nicky Wire of the *Manic Street Preachers* has said, "Wales is a much more complex and divided place than some people think. It isn't this glowing ember of close-knit communities. There's animosity there too."[8] We will seek to identify elements of diversity as well as things held in common.

In order to identify what is distinctive about Wales, six categories will be considered: religion, geography, ethnicity, language and culture, social patterns and political aspiration. These aspects together, in various kaleidoscopic arrangements, make up the contexts of Wales. An understanding of their local combination and expression will be necessary to calibrate mission effectively for a particular community.

8 H. Mackay, "Rugby - an Introduction to Contemporary Wales," in *Understanding Contemporary Wales* (ed. H. Mackay; Cardiff: University of Wales Press, 2010), 6.

The Religious Context of Wales

"The Chapel

A little aside from the main road,
becalmed in a last-century greyness,
there is the chapel, ugly, without the appeal
to the tourist to stop his car
and visit it. The traffic goes by,
and the river goes by, and quick shadows
of clouds, too, and the chapel settles
a little deeper into the grass.

But here once on an evening like this,
in the darkness that was about
his hearers, a preacher caught fire
and burned steadily before them
with a strange light, so that they saw
the splendour of the barren mountains
about them and sang their amens
fiercely, narrow but saved
in a way that men are not now."[9]

Given that Christian mission has a primarily religious motive, the religious aspect of the contexts of Wales will be considered first. This part will consider the origins, growth, decline and legacy of Welsh Nonconformity, and consider the post-Christendom realities that shape mission in Wales in the twenty-first century.

The Origins of Christian Wales

For centuries, the Welsh were regarded, and regarded themselves, as a Christian people.[10] The roots of this have been traced back to Roman

---

9 R. S. Thomas, *Collected Poems 1945 - 1990* (London: Phoenix, 1993), 276. Ronald Stuart Thomas (1913 – 2000) was a Cardiff-born poet and Anglican priest who was a major English language poet of the 20th century. This and subsequent extracts are set out as Thomas published them.
10 Morgan, *Wales and the Word*, 211-213; J. Davies, *A History of Wales* (London: Penguin, 1994), 72-77.

times when the records of the first Christians in Wales can be found. When, however, the pagan Anglo-Saxons migrated from northern Europe, and came to dominate in England, the Christian tradition survived only in the western extremities. The areas under Roman occupation in Wales were not over-run by invaders as the Romans withdrew. South-east Wales remained Roman in culture, and a cradle of the Celtic Church, which then spread to revitalise Europe.

This movement, known as the "Age of the Saints",[11] has been seen as largely independent of Rome and the later Christian activity in England, centred on Canterbury. It gave the Welsh a different Christian identity to the heathen Saxons to the east. Such distinctions may not have been as absolute as the myths they created, but they did have an early influence on identity just at the time when the Welsh were beginning to see themselves as a distinct people, nation and culture.[12] In this way, Christianity became established as a central aspect of Welsh national identity. From AD664 links were made with Canterbury, and for the next thousand years Christianity in Wales was part of Christian Europe, or Christendom. The Reformation did not change things greatly in Wales, and it was not until the early seventeenth century that independent churches of gathered believers, on the Nonconformist model, were established in Wales.[13]

A key factor in the emergence of Welsh Nonconformity, and later Welsh identity, was the translation of the New Testament into Welsh by William Salesbury in 1551, and of the whole Bible by William Morgan in 1588.[14] Morgan's translation and publication was authorised by Elizabeth I as a means to make the Welsh Protestants, and so loyal to the English

---

11 G. Davies, *A Light in the Land: Christianity in Wales 200 - 2000* (Bridgend: Bryntirion, 2002), 16-21.
12 Morgan, *Wales and the Word*, 107, 211.
13 R. T. Jones, *Congregationalism in Wales* (ed. R. Pope; Cardiff: University of Wales Press, 2004), 10-12, 18-19, 21.
14 Davies, *Light*, 49-53; Jones, *Congregationalism*, 8.

government.[15] What was intended as a step along the way to an English-speaking culture and identity did more than anything else to preserve the Welsh language, culture and identity. Indeed, it is unlikely that there would be a Welsh context, distinct from the rest of the United Kingdom, if it were not for Bishop William Morgan's Bible.

The Origins of Welsh Nonconformity

Opinions vary on the growth and strength of the early Nonconformist movement.[16] Some individual churches covered a whole county, with small groups meeting in local villages each week and travelling to meet with other groups less frequently.[17] Churches were small, even when gathered from a wide area, and were linked to similar movements in England.

A little over a hundred years after the publication of William Morgan's Bible, Griffith Jones, the Rector of Llanddowror in Carmarthenshire, started "Circulating Schools" to teach the peasantry of Wales to read. His schools used this Bible as a text book from which to read, memorise and learn, producing a literate, popular culture which would be an outstanding feature of Wales in the nineteenth century. Griffith Jones' motives were evangelistic, but the consequences were also educational, cultural and social, reaching all parts of Wales. By the middle of the nineteenth century, the Welsh were a Welsh-speaking and literate people, with their own, largely Nonconformist, Welsh literature.

The movement's strength in all parts of Wales was largely the result

---

15 E. M. White, *The Welsh Bible* (Stroud: Tempus, 2007), 12, 34, 154; Jones, *Congregationalism*, 52.
16 E. Evans, *Daniel Rowland and the Great Evangelical Awakening in Wales* (Edinburgh: Banner of Truth Trust, 1985), 15; Jones, *Congregationalism*, 34-36, 73, 108-109.
17 R. T. Jones, "Trefniadaeth Ryngeglwysig yr Annibynwyr," *Cofiadur* 21 (Mawrth 1951): 16-30; Jones, *Congregationalism*, 60-78.

of the impact of the Welsh Methodist revival. What started as a renewal movement within the Anglican Church spread through the itinerant preaching of dedicated, dynamic leaders. Those who came to personal faith in Christ through their preaching joined together in small local groups called *seiadau*, for discipleship, accountability and pastoral care.[18] By the nineteenth century, these *seiadau* could be found in most villages and communities in Wales, and became the building blocks of an emerging God-fearing society. They produced a new social order within two generations, spreading a popularist and dynamic Christianity. Recent critics have seen it as a reaction to the rationalism of the age, whereas for those involved it was the result of a revival, an "outpouring of the Blessed Spirit".[19]

The growth and the liveliness of Methodist worship and witness eventually became a threat to the more formal and ordered Nonconformist chapels and leaders, but the sheer scale of Methodist growth and influence could not be resisted. More and more Nonconformist churches, preachers and leaders became "methodised" so that gradually, churches either became as evangelistic and enthusiastic as the Methodists, or they retreated into formalism or the rationalism of Unitarianism.[20]

The Growth of Nonconformist Wales

Welsh was the language medium of all these activities, to the extent that

---

18 G. Tudur, *Howell Harris: From Conversion to Separation 1735 - 1750* (Cardiff: University of Wales Press, 2000), 63-81; E. Evans, *Bread of Heaven: The Life and Work of William Williams, Pantycelyn* (Bridgend: Bryntirion, 2010), 253-261.
19 Evans, *Rowland*, 243; J. M. Jones and W. Morgan, *The Calvinistic Methodist Fathers of Wales* (trans. J. Aaron; Abertawe: Lewis Evans, 1895; repr. Carlisle: Banner of Truth Trust, 2008), 288.
20 Davies, *History*, 337; Jones, *Congregationalism*, 105-107.

Howell Harris could speak of his "Welsh speaking God". [21] The Parish Church, often with a cleric who was unable to speak Welsh, and the dioceses with monoglot and absentee English bishops, were seen as part of the English elite, an impression that has taken centuries to dispel. As a result, the common people, Welsh-speaking in language and culture, increasingly turned to Nonconformity as their spiritual home.

By the nineteenth century this popular movement with nationally known preachers was to sweep all before it. Wales was entering the upheavals of the Industrial Revolution, socially and economically, and Nonconformist Evangelicalism was becoming its dominant religious feature. A series of religious revivals had added thousands to a rapidly growing and multiplying Nonconformity. The Baptist preacher, Christmas Evans, could claim,

> "Perhaps there has never been such a nation as the Welsh who have been won over so widely to the hearing of the gospel. Meeting houses have been erected in each corner of the land and the majority of the common people, nearly all of them, crowd in to listen ... There is virtually no other nation, whose members have, in such numbers, professed the gospel so widely, in both south Wales and the north". [22]

By the time of the 1851 census, there were 2,813 chapels in Wales, with one completed every eight days in the first half of the century. Estimates vary as to what proportion of the 1,163,139 population were Nonconformists, but it has been suggested that 52% attended a place of worship of whom 75% were Nonconformists. However, this did not include those who normally attended places of worship, but were absent

---

21 'God is a Welchman & can talk Welch & has s^d to many in Welch Thy sins are forgiven thee'. Howell Harris Diary 24.5.1770, quoted in E. M. White, "The People Called "Methodists"," *JWRH* 1 (2001): 16.
22 Quoted in Morgan, *Wales and the Word*, 29.

on the day; and some people were counted twice when the services of the day were aggregated.

No doubt the picture was exaggerated by the chapels, for promotional and political reasons, but, nevertheless, the scale of attendance, adherence and influence was out of all proportion to what could have been predicted two generations earlier. By the beginning of the twentieth century, the Nonconformists had 535,000 members, as well an estimated 950,000 adherents who were not members, and half a million children in the Sunday Schools. The proportion of members, adherents and sympathisers in Welsh society meant that evangelism lost its urgency. The chapels were socially and politically active with an array of activities, and Nonconformity had forcibly stamped itself on the Welsh psyche. Wales became known as the "Nonconformist nation", and this myth has left an indelible impression, both positive and negative. The presence of thousands of chapels, whether vibrant, moribund, closing, closed or converted to another use, are a daily reminder in all parts of Wales of a once dominant influence on Welsh society.

The Decline of Nonconformity in Wales

That Welsh Nonconformity's decline occurred so suddenly is as surprising as its rapid rise. The twentieth century began confidently and within four years the prospects looked brighter still. The religious revival of 1904 and 1905 was an international event, and predictions, and subsequent claims, spoke of 100,000 additions to the churches. However, attendances on Sundays were said to be back to pre-revival levels by 1907.[23] The revival's impact on large numbers of people did not prevent

---

23 R. Pope, *Building Jerusalem: Nonconformity, Labour and the Social Question in Wales, 1906 - 1939* (Cardiff: University of Wales Press, 1998), 218-219; R. T. Jones, *Faith and the*

the decline in subsequent decades. Welsh Nonconformity had appeared strong outwardly, but "the corrosive effect of agnosticism, and incipient atheism and general secularisation" were undermining its foundations.[24] The number of people in membership continued to increase until the 1930s, but the numbers attending fell and the non-member "adherents" all but disappeared. Between the end of the Second World War and 1970 the number attending chapels had halved. Nonconformist values that had shaped generations had lost their hold on the people's loyalty and imagination.

By the end of the twentieth century, Nonconformity had been abandoned by the Welsh people, and was entering its death throes. This loss had been regretted even by those who did not attend chapels, because it represented the end of an era, and the loss of something distinctly Welsh. Davies expresses this with evident nostalgia,

> "The Welsh did not revolt against Christianity; rather did they slip from its grasp, and empty chapels were a cause of sadness and regret even to those who never darkened their doors".[25]

Congregations became predominantly middle-aged or elderly. By 2011, the media were speaking of a deteriorating crisis and an approaching end, with decline more rapid than elsewhere in Britain. Chambers expected to see further decline, with only 2% of the chapels open after thirty years that were active at the start of the millennium. There was, he said, "an inevitable feeling that things are coming to an end",[26] with Nonconformist

---

Crisis of a Nation (ed. R. Pope; trans. S. P. Jones; Cardiff: University of Wales, 2004), 348, 362-363, 369.

24 D. Morgan, *The Span of the Cross: Christian Religion and Society in Wales 1914–2000* (Cardiff: University of Wales Press, 1999), 16.

25 Davies, *History*, 642.

26 P. Chambers, "Out of Taste, Out of Time: The Future of Nonconformist Religion in Wales in the Twenty-First Century," *Contemporary Wales* (2008): 87-94.

ministers an "endangered species". As the title of Chambers' article asserts, Welsh Nonconformity was, "Out of Taste and Out of Time".

The reasons given for the demise of historic Welsh Nonconformity have been many. Some saw the decline as the result of changes in Nonconformity itself. Alun Tudur traces the change during the nineteenth century from small family-based groups, meeting in homes and converted barns, to highly organised and professionalised denominations.[27] He shows how the building of chapels produced a respectability that replaced the enthusiasm and relational closeness of early Methodism. By the twentieth century, they represented a formal and passing Victorian culture, "a time-travel capsule into the recent past."[28] This led to a perceived irrelevance among the wider population, and an ill-preparedness to face the future within the chapels. The chapels were seen as captive to a Welsh way of life that was considered antiquated and even hypocritical. Others have linked the decline to the general adoption of Liberal theology,[29] with its social gospel, where personal salvation was down-played. It led to a Church life that did not emphasise evangelism and extension, and without new people joining the Church there was inevitable decline. Others put the decline down to changes in society: English immigration, greater leisure time, rugby, the rise of socialism, or a reaction to the support of the chapels for the First World War.

For many, it was the perceived narrowness of Nonconformity's Puritanism, with a social agenda emphasising teetotalism and sabbatarianism, which led people to turn away. They spoke of the

---

27 A. Tudur, "O'r Sect i'r Enwad: Datblygiad Enwadau Ymneilltuol Cymru, 1840 – 1870" (PhD, Prifysgol Cymru, 1992), 177-197; Jones, *Congregationalism*, 80-81, 151.
28 P. Chambers, *Religion, Secularization and Social Change in Wales* (Cardiff: University of Wales Press, 2005), 73.
29 Morgan, *Span*, 16, 20; Davies, *History*, 505; Chambers, "Out of Taste," 91; Jones, *Faith*, 220-223, 252, 416.

smothering embrace of Welsh Nonconformity. Thomas quotes a variety of authors in a litany of contempt:

> "the dark chapels, squat as toads, raised their faces stonily ... grim fortresses of an oppressive theocracy ... Pompous, bully preachers; lying, lustful, avaricious, hypocritical deacons; morally constipated chapel members; chapel stooges of industrial robber barons ... no nation has come nearer to being a theocracy, a people in vassalage to its preachers ...".[30]

These descriptions may be extreme, but they do reflect an underlying shift in public opinion less than a century after Nonconformity's heyday. The popular mind-set had changed and the prospects for Christian mission had changed with it. This negative legacy is still a major factor in contextualised mission in Wales in the twenty-first century.

Nonconformist Renewal

For some, the revival of 1904 was the "swansong of the old religious tradition of Wales ... the compulsive flush of death".[31] However, for the Evangelical and Pentecostal missions that emerged after the revival, it represented a breath of fresh air and the possibility for a significant break from the traditional and increasingly Liberal older denominations. There was a "problem of wineskins" where the rigidity of the chapels would not, or could not, yield to the new wine. Eifion Evans suggests that most of the initial losses from the chapels were to newly formed "Gospel" or "Mission Halls".[32] Thus, losses to the chapels were not all losses to the Christian community. Indeed, this represented a remarkable church-

---

30 M. W. Thomas, *In the Shadow of the Pulpit: Literature and Nonconformist Wales* (Cardiff: University of Wales Press, 2010), 19, 30, 115.
31 J. G. Jones, "Ebychiad Mawr Olaf Anghydffurfiaeth yng Nghymru," *Cymmrodorion* 11 (2005): 134.
32 E. Evans, *The Welsh Revival of 1904* (Port Talbot: Evangelical Movement of Wales, 1969), 186.

planting movement. As one convert put it, "Those who have been born in the fire cannot live in the smoke".

Some of the "Children of the Revival" were hoping for a return to apostolic Christianity. They started to set up Pentecostal Missions, either out of or alongside the Gospel Halls. The link between the revival and the early Pentecostal movement was more inspirational than a direct cause, though it had been "rocked in the cradle of little Wales" according to Bartleman, one of Pentecostalism's first leaders. Jones saw the revival as the "starting point of an immense spiritual movement", in that the worldwide Pentecostal movement, with its millions of members, was a direct outcome.[33]

Because the Evangelical and Pentecostal churches in Wales often comprised small congregations, they were disregarded by the Nonconformist denominations, which were much larger. However, as decline in the larger denominations set in, some Evangelical and Pentecostal churches began to strengthen and plant new churches. This was accelerated when numbers of evangelically minded churches, leaders, and members seceded from the denominations in the 1960s over the Ecumenical Movement or the Charismatic Movement. By the end of the century, these churches were the largest churches in Wales, and growing, especially in the towns and cities. This was part of what Bebbington calls "The Evangelical Resurgence in the Later Twentieth Century".[34]

The Changing Religious Context

The number of people describing themselves as "Christian" in Wales in the 2001 and 2011 censuses fell from 72% to 57.6% of the population.

---

33 Jones, *Faith*, 337-349.
34 D. W. Bebbington, *Evangelicalism in Modern Britain* (London: Routledge, 1999), 249-270.

The 2007 *Tearfund* survey, however, gives a more telling and bleak picture.[35] The respondents were divided into three main categories: "churchgoers", "non-churched' and "de-churched". These represent those who go (however occasionally), those who have never gone, and those who used to go but no longer do so. 20% responded as churchgoers, 28% as non-churched, but 51% as de-churched. The latter reflects Wales' disenchantment with religion and the percentage of de-churched is significantly higher than the other nations of the United Kingdom. More than half of those polled in Wales said that they used to have links with places of worship but no longer did so. Nearly three-quarters said that they were closed to the possibility of attendance in the future. Mission in Wales in the twenty-first century is mission in a post-Christian, even anti-Christian, context, a sphere described by missiologists as Post-Christendom.

Secularism, materialism, and post-modernity have affected and taken expression in Wales. For the churches, the demise of Christendom is even more significant. It had assumed a nominally Christian population that needed to be drawn into church buildings. In its ministry, the office of pastor and teacher completely eclipsed that of apostle and evangelist. Evangelism, where it occurred, was what Hirsch calls "outreach and grab" or "outreach and amuse", being a centripetal movement into church buildings and community.[36] This was an attractional and extractional model rather than a missional and outreach model.[37] For Hirsch, faith was expressed within the church's buildings, rather than in the wider community.[38] This meant that mission involved encouraging people to go

---

35 *Tearfund*, "Church Going in the UK," 11. http://news.bbc.co.uk/1/shared/bsp/hi/pdfs/03_04_07_tearfundchurch.pdf
36 A. Hirsch, *The Forgotten Ways* (Grand Rapids: Brazos, 2006), 34, 60, 65, 129-130, 220, 276.
37 S. Murray, *Church After Christendom* (Milton Keynes: Paternoster, 2004), 21-22.
38 Hirsch, *Forgotten*, 238.

to chapel, rather than a mission by the people into their community.

The churches are no longer operating in a society that accepts a Christian worldview,[39] and, as a result, the Church in the West is suffering from "future shock", in that the Church was struggling to adjust to its strange new world. Aspirations, such as Newbigin's "claiming the high ground of public truth", or desires to convert the culture, will need to guard against an unconscious attempt to re-impose a cultural Christendom. In a post-Christendom context, the Christendom models, methods and privileges are not transferable. If Christendom assumptions are not abandoned, current trends of decline will only continue.[40] In a pre-Christendom society, Christianity was fresh news, proclaimed as an alternative religious and social option. In a post-Christendom society, Christianity can all too easily be seen as passé, irrelevant and old fashioned, with little to offer. It is seen as having been tried and found wanting, and those looking for answers to contemporary questions require new answers. For these reasons, the missional challenge in twenty-first century Wales will need to be viewed through a post-Christendom lens. Chambers, however, suggests that high levels of religious pluralism do not necessarily lead to lower levels of church attendance or religious belief. He sees the decline of institutional religion as creating an opportunity for the continuance and growth of mission orientated churches.[41]

In Section Two we will consider how effectively the six *Approaches* to mission adjusted to the new religious context, and in Section Three we will draw lessons and strategies for the future.

---

39 T. J. Keller, *Center Church* (Grand Rapids: Zondervan, 2012), 181-182.
40 Murray, *Church After Christendom*, 24, 39-45.
41 Chambers, *Religion*, 38.

The Geographic Context of Wales

"Boundaries

Where does the town end
And the country begin?

Where is the high-water mark
Between the grey tide and the green?

We walk an invisible margin remembering glory ..."[42]

Welshness, and any consideration of Welsh contexts, will refer in part to the land, the territory, the region within fixed borders that define Wales. An awareness or experience of Wales is inseparable from a sense of place. The shape of the land and its geology have affected the history, society, politics, economy and identity of Wales and the Welsh.

Those who were born within the boundaries of Wales, or are descended from those who were, would normally consider themselves to be Welsh. It is being born in the land, not living in it, that creates Welshness. National identity involves a community of some sort within a definite social space, "a fairly well demarcated and bounded territory, with which the members identify and to which they feel they belong".[43]

Unlike Scotland or Ireland, this boundary in Wales is not made up entirely of sea or mountain range. The "Welsh peninsula" to the west of England has not been regarded as fully national because its geography

---

42 R. S. Thomas, *Collected Later Poems: 1988 - 2000* (Tarset: Bloodaxe, 2004), 258.
43 A. D. Smith, *National Identity* (London: Penguin, 1991), 9.

left it open to domination and incursion from the east. The valleys of the Severn, Dee and Wye rivers flowing east provide valley routes, for culture as well as intruders, into the centre of the central massif which dominates the land area.

However, remoteness from the centre of English power helped preserve a separate language, culture and identity. Nevertheless, it was a man-made construction that probably secured a distinct identity for the Welsh. Offa, king of Wessex, built a dyke, a palisaded wall of earth and upright wood, to defend against raids from the west in the eighth century.[44] In so doing, he penned off diverse Celtic tribes and helped unite these remnants of the old Brythonic tribal stock into a distinct people. Because of the separation it produced, the Welsh beyond the wall developed an identity of exclusion: they knew who they were "by knowing who you are not". The label, "Welsh" is from the Saxon, "Wealh", meaning "foreigner", whereas the word the Welsh used to describe themselves was "Cymro", meaning "comrade". The contrasting labels well illustrate the psychological influence of Offa's dyke. This border, and the land it separates, thus created a sense of national place which was reinforced by maps, population censuses, and collective institutions. Together, they contributed to the building of an imagined nation and identity, to use Anderson's graphic term.[45]

The Patchwork of Regions

Mike Perrin describes the different regions of Wales as the "anvil upon which the Welsh nation has been forged and fashioned." [46] The central

44 Davies, *History*, 64-66, 80.
45 B. Anderson, *Imagined Communities: Reflections on the Origins and Spread of Nationalism* (London: Verso, 1991), 6.
46 M. Perrin, *From Shore to Shore* (Bridgend: Bryntirion, 2000), 17.

massif not only separated the various Celtic tribes, but also resulted in poor communication between Wales' regions. This led to a lack of national unity, but was also the ideal refuge for guerrilla-fighters defending the land. It has been said that "English stamina simply failed beyond about 600 feet", which led to incomplete invasions and the need for repeated conquests.

For the most part, the climate is wet, the soils poor, the terrain difficult, and what good land there is, is on the margins and rarely extensive. The people existed by adapting to a largely poor upland environment. The geography shaped social practice so that the Welsh could be depicted by Day as a "marginal people in a marginal land, clinging on heroically against enormous odds – both natural and man-made".[47] Until the nineteenth century, Wales had few towns, and is, to this day, a nation of villages and small towns, a "community of communities".[48] What the land did have, however, was a number of lucrative regions with all the resources needed for coal and steel production. These fired the Industrial Revolution and brought mass immigration from other parts of the British Isles.

Balsom suggests a "Three-Wales Model",[49] in which Wales transitions, west to east, from "*y Fro Gymraeg*" (i.e. a Welsh-speaking rural culture); to "Welsh Wales" (i.e. the English-speaking former industrial areas); to "British Wales" (i.e. the areas adjacent to or shaped by their English / British-ness). A mosaic of regions is home to just over three million people, a large proportion of whom live in villages or small towns. Upland features still separate areas and communities, making travel protracted and circuitous. Economic developments divided the rural from the

---

47 Day, *Making Sense*, 16.
48 G. Day, "Place and Belonging," in *Understanding Contemporary Wales* (ed. H. Mackay; Cardiff: University of Wales Press, 2010), 43.
49 D. Balsom, "The Three-Wales Model," in *The National Question Again* (ed. J. Osmond; Llandysul: Gomer, 1985), 1-17.

industrial, not least by the languages spoken. Geographical factors have shaped Welsh culture, society and the communities that Christian mission seeks to engage with.

Rural and industrial landscapes reflect two images of Wales, though aspects of one are often found in the other, in specific local communities. Pictures of rural communities, of sheep, mountains and small tranquil villages have endured as images of Wales, but underlying depopulation, deprivation and demographic change increasingly reflected rural communities in crisis. At the same time, three quarters of the population of Wales live on a third of the land, so images of the industrial Valleys have become dominant. Industrialisation developed widely throughout the nineteenth century, but the rapid expansion of coal extraction in Glamorgan drew the rural population on an unprecedented scale. The dramatic and exploitative transformation from a rural to an industrial environment was what Cordell called the "Rape of the Fair Country".

The heyday of Welsh industrialisation, however, passed, and the decline of extraction industries was almost as rapid as their expansion had been. In the twentieth century, images of urban solidarity, as well as rural harmony, were replaced by decline, unemployment and deprivation. A third of manufacturing jobs were lost between 1979 and 1983, leaving a largely low-paid service economy. This has led to a loss of individual self-confidence and an undermining of community identity. Nicky Wire, of the *Manic Street Preachers*, who grew up in the former industrial Valleys described them as "morbidly angry".[50]

---

50 C. Sullivan, "Wales," *Guardian* (15.02.2008).

Gwladgarwch and *Brogarwch*

The variety and multiplicity of regions and communities in Wales, and their separation from each other, has led to a strong awareness of, and loyalty to, place. Throughout the centuries, Welsh loyalties have been local. Individuals are defined by their place, and often the first question asked is, "Where are you from?", so that their home or locality is a greater signifier than their surname. The Welsh national anthem does not refer to the British monarch but to the *gwlad*, the land. The Welsh people have a love and loyalty to this national land, *gwladgarwch*, but especially to the particular locality of their upbringing, *brogarwch*. *Gwladgarwch* is evident in international relations or rugby matches, but it is a development, a composite, in which people feel they belong to a national community, based on their local loyalties. The local loyalty has always been more important than that of nation. *"Bro"* is described as an "evocative word", meaning a person's "place", "section of valley", village, landscape, district or region. This localism shapes how individuals view and experience their national identity through ordinary social relations and experiences. It is the basis of the Welsh *hiraeth*, or longing for home, expressed by those living away.

That Wales is a mosaic of different localities, economies, environments and regions means that the features of one geographical context cannot be said to be true of all. The variety will call for a localism in approaches to mission. How effective the different *Approaches* have been in this adjustment will be seen in Chapter Two, so that appropriate strategies can be considered in Section Three.

The Ethnic Context
of Wales

"Reservoirs"[51]

There are places in Wales I don't go:
Reservoirs that are the subconscious
Of a people, troubled far down
With gravestones, chapels, villages even;
The serenity of their expression
Revolts me, it is a pose
For strangers, a watercolour's appeal
To the mass, instead of the poem's
Harsher conditions ...

Where can I go, then, from the smell
Of decay, from the putrefying of a dead
Nation? I have walked the shore
For an hour and seen the English
Scavenging among the remains
Of our culture, covering the sand
Like the tide and, with the roughness
Of the tide, elbowing our language
Into the grave that we have dug for it."

Whether or not a people have an actual or an imagined ethnicity, the perception of it will affect them and any mission to their context. The term 'ethnic', from the Greek word for 'nation', $\grave{\epsilon}\theta\nu\eta$, was adopted by sociologists in its French form, *ethnie*, to convey a sense of kinship, shared culture and solidarity. It involves a sense of "us" as opposed to "them", usually being expressed in a shared name, homeland, culture, solidarity, or myths and memories of origin and history. Ideas of ethnicity have been expressed in different ways, but they tend to emphasise two main categories. A "primordialist" interpretation seeks to trace the literal descent of a people from pre-historical times, and a "social constructionist" position looks at a people's assumed ethnicity.

---

51 Thomas, *Poems 1945-1990*, 194.

Wales' Celtic Past

Early history and myth claimed that the Welsh were part of a Celtic or Brythonic people who originated in central Europe, or even southern Hindustan. Cato the Elder, 234-149 BC, identified the Celts as delighting in both fighting well and speaking well, more than anything else. Gerald of Wales, in the twelfth century, speaks of the Welsh people's distinctive respect for fighting prowess, family, hospitality, egalitarianism, and love of singing. The perceived distinctives of Welsh people, including "Celtic melancholy" or "Celtic fire", are markers said to derive from Welsh forebears.

This view of Welsh distinctiveness was, in no small part, based on the record of the sixth century historian Gildas. He claimed that various Celtic tribes had occupied the whole of Britain, throughout the Roman occupation, until the movement of Anglo-Saxon peoples from northern Europe into England. He described this movement of people as on such a scale that the Celts were pushed west and north, losing all territory apart from the "Celtic fringe" of the British Isles, notably Ireland, Cornwall, Wales, Scotland, and northern England. The Welsh word for the English remains *Saeson* [i.e. Saxon] to this day. The building of Offa's dyke penned these tribes in, and, with a separate language and culture, they preserved a largely separate ethnicity until the inward migration of recent centuries. This view of history asserted a racial distinction between the Welsh and their neighbours. It was reinforced by a distinct language and culture, and justified a sense of grievance for the "lost lands" to the east as well as many perceived threats from that source, to liberty, culture, prosperity and even survival. The Welsh *ethnie* was thus perceived as an embattled and exploited people of ancient descent.

Such a view of history held force until the 1960s when its basic assumptions were questioned. As a result, it was concluded that the size of the Anglo-Saxon movement of peoples into Britain was on a much smaller scale, akin to the Norman conquest of the eleventh century. Here, a dominant class gradually took over the levers of power, bringing some of its language and culture, but largely integrating with the existing peoples of what became England. This view suggested that the Welsh people were the same stock as their neighbours, and so enhanced an awareness of a shared Britishness. The Welsh were Welsh because they "invented themselves", to use Williams' stark phrase.[52] They could choose a Welsh, English or British identity, and their awareness and culture would be shaped accordingly.

The revisionist view was politically popular from a British perspective as it largely undermined a primordalist view of a distinct Welsh ethnicity. However, this view has also come in for serious questioning. It fails to explain the almost total absence of Welsh/ Brythonic words in the English language, or the absence of Brythonic settlements and artifacts from the conquest period onwards. The main rebuttal, however, has occurred as a result of recent research into the human genome. Markers on the male Y chromosome are passed down through each male generation without alteration and therefore show the regional origins of particular peoples. Studies by Thomas, *et al*, have shown a clear genetic distinction between the settled populations of England and Wales, with a gradual transition along the border with England.[53] The Welsh, according to Weale, are more closely related to the Basque peoples of northern Spain than their English neighbours.[54] It is suggested that this reflects the pre-historic migration

---

52 Williams, *When was Wales*, 2.
53 C. Capelli et al., "A Y Chromosome Census of the British Isles," *CURR BIOL* 13 (11 2003): 979, 983. Online: http://www.freewebs.com/flanneryclandna/PDFPAPERS/YCAPELLI2003.pdf; Weale et al., "Y Chromosome Evidence," 1018.
54 Weale et al., "Y Chromosome Evidence," 1009.

of peoples living on the western European seaboard, and subsequent trading contacts, not a merging with people from the east. Since the Celtic migrations, however, further immigration and emigration have made the picture less clear, blurring the genetic distinction.

The Effects of Immigration and Emigration

The conquest of lowland Wales by the Normans and Edward I, and its annexation by Henry VIII, facilitated the migration of the non-Welsh into the more accessible and profitable parts of Wales. The coming of the Romans, the establishing of Norman lordships in the south and along the border, the settlement of Flemish people in southern Pembrokeshire, and the establishment of urban and rural "Englishries" around Edward's castles, introduced a diversity of peoples into Wales. It meant that the productive lands of the south, and the first towns in Wales, were English in character and language, as well as being the centres of power and legislation. The Welsh were considered as "foreigners" in such towns. This produced "Welshries", or areas of Welsh loyalty, language and culture, and centuries of struggle against the "other", not just over the border, but now within.

When industrialisation began in the eighteenth and nineteenth centuries, the needed labour pool was initially drawn from the rural areas, where living standards and income were even lower than in the squalor of the emerging extraction towns producing coal and slate. However, by the second half of the nineteenth century, labour was being drawn into Wales, mostly from England and Ireland. The population grew from just over half a million at the beginning of the nineteenth century to 2.5 million in 1911. By 1891, one in seven of the population had moved from England, with 121,653 into Glamorgan alone. By the 2011 census, 27% of residents in Wales had been born elsewhere, but this movement was to rural not industrial areas. In rural areas, the proportions of those from across the border were higher: Anglesey 29%, Gwynedd 33%, Denbigh 36%, Ceredigion 37%, Conwy 40%, and Powys 45%. Immigration, especially to rural areas, is seen by the resident population as a threat to traditional cultures, language and stability. The indigenous population thus sought to build social barriers against the ideas of "English affluence, arrogance and insensitivity".[55] People from the urban centres of England were looking for a better environment for life, and "converting rural areas into middle-class enclaves". The trend has been referred to as "rural retreating",[56] or in the case of the elderly as "geriatric infill", the coast becoming "Costa Geriatrica". House prices rose as a result, beyond what was affordable for young local families. This was exacerbated by the purchasing of property as holiday homes, which led to the arson campaign of the 1970s.[57] These, with other grievances, led to a rise in nationalism in Wales.

The situation was also affected by people moving to England. In 2011, 506,619 people born in Wales were living in England. In the time of the inter-war depression, Wales was the only part of the United Kingdom where the population actually fell. A grave in Trealow reads, "not dead but gone to Slough". Day speaks of a tragic-comedy in which "so many brought up here want to get out and so many not brought up here want to get in".[58] Ethnic hostility to "incomers" has been the result.

Welsh Identity and Ethnicity

If the first question asked when meeting Welsh people relates to where

---

55 Day, *Making Sense*, 179.
56 Carter, *Against the Odds*, 76.77.
57 Carter, *Against the Odds*, 86.
58 Day, *Making Sense*, 183.

in Wales they originate, the second would ask to whom they were related, genealogy being a common interest. This, in part, derives from the law code of Hywel Dda, the tenth century law-maker and king of Deheubarth in south-west Wales, who required families to know their lineage for nine generations, for compensation in cases of murder. A Welsh person's lineage proved his belonging to a distinct tribe, and was encouraged by perceived connections to a wider family of Celtic peoples.

It made the *ethnie* central to personal, family and national identity, and has been used for cultural and political reasons. The controversy over a Welsh tick-box, prior to the 2001 Census, demonstrated a desire in many to declare their distinctiveness. The 2011 Census recorded the respondent's view of their own identity, where more than one marker could be selected. For Wales as a whole 57.5% described themselves as "Welsh" only, 7.1% as "Welsh" and "British", 16.9% as "British" only, 11.2% as "English" only, and 1.5% as "English" and "British". However, regional variations showed considerable differences and reflect different factors:

- In the border county of Powys the scale of cross-border migration (44.7% born in England), and the strength of Britishness, are seen in the responses. 28.8% of the population described themselves as British in some way, whereas less than half of the population describe themselves as Welsh.

- In Anglesey, part of the heartland area of the Welsh language (57.2% Welsh-speaking), the effect of inward migration to the coastal and tourist areas is also evident (28.8% born in England). Two distinct communities exist. The proportion speaking Welsh is equivalent to those who identified themselves as Welsh in terms of identity, and English / British is the identity of the 30% of the population born outside of Wales.

- In the county of Rhondda Cynon Taf, at the head of one of the post-industrial Valleys of south Wales, the awareness of Welsh identity is the highest of any region at 73.3% of the population, even though only 12% claim to speak Welsh. This identity of Welshness is based on location, not language, and the absence of inward migration from England is evident.

Such measures of identity, however, do not necessarily support a primordialist or a constructionist ethnic root to a person's sense of identity, but they do show degrees of "otherness" from their English neighbours. The genetic research by Thomas, Weale *et al.*, does demonstrate an element of primordialist *ethnie*, especially in one of the sample areas in central Anglesey, where the indigenous population was Welsh-speaking and had been less affected by inward migration. In other areas, such as Merthyr Tydfil, the *ethnie* of Welshness was a construction, despite large-scale inward migration during the massive population growth of the industrial era. It was a perceived or imagined identity, but strong nonetheless. Being the *Cymry*, the comrades, as opposed to being English or British, forms a significant distinctive of identity and context.

The extent to which Welsh ethnicity, as part of Welsh identity, is historically based or imagined, will matter little in terms of any missional response to it. The Welsh may be mongrels and hybrids, but any claim to a distinct *ethnie*, by an individual or a community, is none the less influential. The degree to which a local population see themselves as ethnically distinct will need to be calibrated in effective mission. How effective the different *Approaches* have been in finding Welsh solutions, patterns, and even Welsh-born leaders will be seen in Chapter Two, so that appropriate models can be considered in Section Three.

The Linguistic and Cultural Context of Wales

"The Old Language

England, what have you done to make the speech

My fathers used a stranger at my lips,

An offence to the ear, a shackle on the tongue

That would fit new thoughts to an abiding tune?

Answer me now. ... When spring wakens the hearts

Of the young children to sing, what song shall be theirs?"[59]

The consequence of Offa's dyke was to define a geographical entity, and to give a boundary to the Celtic peoples who were located, for the most part, behind it. However, the most significant difference that the boundary marked was that of language. The Brythonic language that had predominated in northern and western England developed into Welsh around the eighth century, and those who spoke it were eventually located exclusively in the land area now known as Wales. The other areas with Brythonic languages akin to Welsh (Cornwall, southern Scotland and the north of England) gradually succumbed to the English language and regional forms of Englishness.

The distinct language in Wales, with a largely monoglot population, gave particular expression to the sense of "other" from the English. It was the most obvious badge of Welsh identity, and differentiated Wales from all its neighbours. For this reason, the language became the key marker of context and identity for Wales and the Welsh for the thousand years prior to the twentieth century. It also isolated the Welsh socially, culturally and

---

59 A. Thwaite, ed., *R. S. Thomas* (London: Everyman, 1996), 18.

politically until commerce, invasion and immigration produced English-speaking areas and influence. Its historical continuity makes it one of the oldest spoken languages in Europe.[60]

In the Acts of Union, of 1536 and 1543, Wales was incorporated into England, making its people subjects of the English Crown. The Union was an official attempt to enforce uniformity within the realm, including the destruction of the language. It debarred Welsh speakers from public office and provided all judicial and administrative functions in English only. It was followed by a desire in England that the "British language may be quite extinct and may be English'd out of Wales".[61] In 1847 a government report into education in Wales, known as *Brad y Llyfrau Gleision (The Treachery of the Blue Books)*, claimed that schools in Wales were inadequate, largely because of the continuing influence of the Welsh language and Sunday schools. A furore resulted, but a lasting impression was made that Welsh was a primitive and backward language, and that self-improvement required the wholesale adoption of English. Parents increasingly spoke English to their children in order to help them to "get on". Welsh was banned from the school system and those caught speaking it had to wear the "Welsh Not", and the person wearing it at the end of the school day was thrashed. Matthew Arnold, writing in the Times on 8th September, 1866, said,

> "The Welsh language is the curse of Wales. Its prevalence, and the ignorance of English have excluded, and even now exclude, the Welsh people from the civilisation of their neighbours ... The sooner all Welsh specialists disappear from the face of the Earth, the better".[62]

---

60 Day, *Making Sense*, 22; Jones, *Desire*, 73, 90.
61 M. Parker, *Neighbours from Hell? English Attitudes to the Welsh* (Talybont: Lolfa, 2007), 50.
62 Carter, *Against the Odds*, 61.

The collective memory of these events, among Welsh-speaking communities, has left a legacy of bitterness to the present day. The attacks on the language influenced the Welsh psyche by undermining the confidence of Welsh speakers, and by creating a siege mentality. Dr Dilys Davies, a senior psychologist advising the Welsh Assembly Government, explains the psychological effect of English colonialism on cultural and national identity, and calls for special health provision to respond to it.[63]

The Decline of the Language

Despite English opposition to the language, and the immigration of English speakers, the number of Welsh speakers in Wales continued to grow in the nineteenth century. It reached a peak of 977,366 in 1911, which was about half the population. From 1911 to 1971, however, each 10-year census has shown a decline in every age group. The reasons for the decline are complex, but inward migration, parental aspirations for the perceived advantages of speaking English, and the economic and social influence of the British state were powerful factors. At the beginning of the twentieth century, the areas where the language was spoken had diminished. There were three corridors running north to south: the eastern section becoming entirely English-speaking, and the west was mostly Welsh. By the end of the century, this had broken down further into a patchwork of small language areas. The areas of *y Fro Gymraeg*, where community life was conducted in Welsh, were shrinking rapidly. By the time of the 2011 census, Welsh had become a minority language in all but Anglesey and Gwynedd.

---

63 D. Davies, *Speaking the Invisible* (Felinfach: All Wales Network Committee for Arts Therapies Professions, 2002), Online: http://www.wales.nhs.uk/sites3/documents/415/Speaking-the-Invisible.pdf. 37-42.

For political nationalists, the survival of the language, and the culture it nurtures, was essential to the future of Wales as an entity, as "if the language goes, Wales as such would cease to be".[64] One of the founders of *Plaid Cymru*, Saunders Lewis, in an influential speech, *Tynged yr Iaith* (Fate of the Language) in 1962, argued that protecting and preserving culture was more important than achieving political autonomy because the latter depended on the former.[65] Lewis's call for direct action to preserve the language and the culture led to the founding of *Cymdeithas yr Iaith Gymraeg* (The Welsh Language Society) whose direct action has done much to influence the National Assembly's Welsh language policy. Llewellyn spoke of Welshness dying with the language as "population recomposition" by English inward migration reduced Welsh areas: "every time a home in *Y Fro Gymraeg* goes to a foreigner we die, every time a young Welshman leaves *Y Fro Gymraeg* we die ... our Country, Wales, has ceased to be".[66] The language issue had produced a "fortress Wales" mind-set and a call for "ethnic cleansing" in which Welsh homes were to be returned to Welsh speakers.[67] The rightness of such issues is a matter of debate, but that they impinge on approaches to Welsh language contexts is self-evident.

A slowing of these trends can be seen because of the influence of the growth of Welsh medium education, especially by the children of English-speaking homes attending Welsh-medium schools. Projections of an upward trend can be drawn, provided that those leaving Welsh-medium education continue to speak Welsh in adulthood. If this is the case, the number of Welsh speakers in all age groups will increase to the proportion

---

64 Day, *Making Sense*, 23.
65 S. Lewis, "Tynged yr Iaith," Online: http://quixoticquisling.com/testun/saunders-lewis-fate-of-the-language.html .
66 Quoted in Day, *Making Sense*, 213.
67 Day, *Making Sense*, 214.

of those speaking Welsh during school age. This trend is supported by the equal status given to Welsh by law in a bilingual society, which has "normalised" the language as a means of communication. It has also been strengthened by vibrant Welsh language media. The language is vulnerable, but no longer threatened and inevitably declining. In terms of mission context, the linguistic makeup of Wales is expected, therefore, to change over the first half of the twenty-first century.

The Welsh Cultural Tradition and the Language

Language is more than a means of communication; it is also a cultural medium. It shapes the rituals, social relations and values of the society framed by it.[68] Because of this, the language and culture of a people are inseparable. The place of song and choral singing, mentioned by Gerald of Wales, still gives a popular expression to this poetic tradition. Nicky Wire, of the *Manic Street Preachers*, in explaining the rise of Welsh singing groups claimed, "But one thing about our domain of south Wales is that everybody can sing. That's our national identity ... the emphasis on singing is almost like a trade here". The poetic and choral tradition had enjoyed a renaissance in the nineteenth century through the reinvention of the *eisteddfod*, held locally, regionally and nationally.[69] These became "a showcase for Welshness", and, through their competitions, "a one-nation Olympic games of the mind".[70]

Trends which established Welsh as an increasingly urban language have also strengthened the language. Welsh language film, television, theatre, and live rugby commentary, have redefined the image and given the language new prospects. This "Cool Cymru" represents a new Welsh

---

68 Carter, *Against the Odds*, 17.
69 R. T. Jones, *The Desire of Nations* (Llandybie: Christopher Davies, 1974), 153; Day, *Making Sense*, 21.
70 E. Humphreys, *The Taliesin Tradition* (Bridgend: Seren, 1989), 128, 132, 142.

culture: sophisticated, secular, post-Christian, and professional. In a bilingual society, Welsh-speaking professionals found unprecedented opportunities, a success that has led to envy and resentment in some non-Welsh speakers.

The Language as a Marker or Cause of Division

For many living in Wales, their sense of identity was a cultural matter, shaped by language, religion, customs and images. For them, Welsh identity "cannot be sustained by rugby, choirs and laverbread". However, as the number of Welsh speakers declined, the role of the language in shaping identity began to be challenged and rejected. As communities became wholly English-speaking, the language became a divisive issue, making those who did not speak Welsh feel like second class citizens, or not really Welsh at all. In the post-industrial south Wales Valleys, the population reacted and opposed the language and the nationalist movement. They felt excluded from the rural culture of north and west Wales, and the *Eisteddfod*, and even if they regretted their lack, the issue drove a wedge of exclusion through Welsh culture, society and identity. Those speaking Welsh, with better job opportunities because of bilingualism, were suspected of a form of cultural elitism. Some English language media, and many of the anglicised population, objected to bilingual government forms and an imposed, and artificially revived, Welshness. They also portrayed *Cymdeithas yr Iaith Gymraeg* as "The Welsh Taliban".[71] A Western Mail article in February, 1968, declared the need for Wales to be English-speaking, insisting that identity was not dependant on the language. The language, as a marker, had become a symbol of division rather than national identity, a challenge to the genuineness of the Welshness of non-Welsh speakers, not a symbol of it. In the Labour Force Survey of 2001,

---

71 R. Lewis, "The Tyranny of the Welsh Taliban," Daily Mail. 15.01.13.

the south Wales Valleys recorded the highest level of Welsh identity of all the regions of Wales, but based on place of birth and rugby loyalty, not language and traditional culture.[72] This form of Welshness was expressed in accents, flags, anthems, and the social warmth of "Gavin and Stacey". Welshness, from this perspective, has been described as "an attitude of mind – sometimes psychopathic, often generous, usually friendly, and always passionate". These images are what Anderson saw as the ingredients of an "imagined community", an invention of a community of people, expressed by Catatonia's declaration, "Every day when I wake up. I thank the Lord I'm Welsh", or by the unity engendered by a Welsh victory on the rugby field.

The icons and images of culture, be they language, sport, music or literature, are present to different degrees in the various regional expressions of Welshness. In many ways the local context, as well as the culture, will be defined by them.

An approach to mission in one area may be appropriate or alien, depending on the context. In predominantly Welsh-speaking areas, English language churches will be viewed as a further form of colonisation. Chambers speaks of a "cultural lag" that results in Welsh language churches choosing not to adjust to changes in their own culture and community.[73] Such chapels are caught in a time-warp, in a culture that has changed fundamentally. Rowan Williams commented pointedly that "Welsh has reinvented itself, but Welsh-speaking Christianity largely has not".

Section Two will show how sensitively and effectively the various *Approaches* have made their adjustments. Section Three will suggest how this might be done effectively.

---

72 Carter, *Against the Odds*, 106.
73 Chambers, *Religion*, 70-71.

The Social Context
of Wales

"He lives here
> and a pulpit grew up under my feet
> And I climbed into it and

It was a cage

of the mine-shaft down down down
>> to preach to the lost souls
>> of the coal-face reminding

how green is the childhood
>> of a glib people taunting
> them with the abandonment
> of the national for the class struggle."[74]

The influence of the physical geography of Wales was that communities were small and often isolated. Welsh communities developed in a scattered and intimate way, where migration was limited and extended families became the matrix of the community. *Brogarwch* took priority over *gwladgarwch,* in that a person's locality meant even more to them than their nationality, and Wales has been described as a "community of communities" as a result.

Under an Anglicised aristocracy was a mass of rural labouring people, without a middle class, and with a culture determined by language and its resulting isolation from the influence of external forces. The non-stratified nature of Welsh society had also been influenced, over centuries, by the practice of partible inheritance, where, after death, an estate was divided evenly between male heirs, in contrast to the English system where the

---

74 R. S. Thomas, *What is a Welshman?* (Llandybie: Christopher Davies, 1974), 1.

eldest son received the whole. Estates were constantly dividing, thus largely preventing dynastic families from ruling large areas, and inevitably leading to a history of sibling strife. This made Wales harder to govern, but also harder to conquer, as no one leader represented the whole.[75] These factors produced distinct social patterns in relation to family, community and social structure.

The *Gwerin*

Rural isolation, and the insular nature of the industrial Valleys, separated from each other by hill ranges, produced familiarity and cohesion within communities. The people were the *gwerin*, the Welsh folk, living off the land by their labour, the "heart and soul of the Welsh nation who cultivated a respectable and genial commonality".[76] The Welsh word, *gwerin*, means "a mass", and refers to a supposed homogeneous body of people. Social life centred on the *aelwyd*, the hearth, where socialisation, education and organisation were grounded. *Teulu ni*, our family, was the basis of identity, loyalty, and genealogical roots. The society provided its people with values and stability. Jones describes these family-focussed values:

> "Kindness, good deeds, thrift, hospitality, generosity towards the poor, and diligence - all these had a place of honour in the pattern. Family life was to be respected and although unchastity among young unmarried folk was tolerated, and while the illegitimate child was usually treated with great kindness, adultery was considered inexcusable. Mothers were given unprecedented respect and children were increasingly treated with ıderness."[77]

gainst the Odds, 222.
When was Wales, 237-238.
62.

A strong sense of kinship and localism inevitably produced an awareness of local belonging and inter-dependence. In addition to cooperation within the extended family, from medieval times, farmers and neighbours provided an agricultural mutual aid, known as *cymhortha* (from the verb "to help"). This system of goodwill and co-operation facilitated community development and survival. In the same spirit, the provision of hospitality for strangers was expected. This communalism and mutualism produced a society in which every member was important. A visitor attending a funeral commented, "Everybody turns out for funerals around here. At first I thought it must be someone important, then I realised that everyone in the village was important".

This image of an egalitarian society was further developed during the Nonconformist era, when everyone in the chapels were supposed to be equal before God, with farm labourers sharing the deacons' pew with their employer. The *gwerin* was the basic form of politics, expressing democratic and even republican ideas in the *gweriniaeth*, the rule of the *gwerin*. The political link with Liberalism, and influence on it, resulted.

The Welsh Socialist Tradition

These essentially rural patterns were not lost when industrialisation drew the workforce from the fields to the furnaces and coal-face. In the industrial Valleys, the egalitarian society was on a much larger scale, and developed into "religious socialism", but was no less communal and mutual. The mining communities were extracting both coal and slate in dangerous conditions, and survived by mutual self-reliance. Among the working poor, socialist principles gathered popularity, initially within the chapels and later distinct from them. Loyalty to the Liberal Welsh politics of Lloyd George began to give way to the socialism of Keir Hardie, when

Hardie became the MP for Merthyr Tydfil in 1900. This socialism was English-speaking, British or Internationalist in sympathy, and increasingly secular.

For the next hundred years of industrial uncertainty, there was a wholesale loyalty to the Labour Party in the Welsh coalfields. In political terms, Wales became "Labour-Land", with socialism in its DNA and across its social strata. Labour became the "party of the *gwerin*", but a *gweriniaeth* less defined than its Nonconformist precursor.

By the end of the century, the chapels and the mines were closing rapidly, and the post-industrial Valleys were losing their cohesiveness. Social crises multiplied in family life, education, and law and order. Drug abuse, social exclusion and hopelessness produced a social underclass in the post-industrial areas. Such a legacy of industrial decline is in marked contrast to the rising prosperity of the coastal cities. These extremes marked the end of any semblance of an egalitarian, classless Welsh society, the *gwerin*.

Rugby as a Social Unifier

It has been argued that Welsh communal egalitarianism is more evident in the nation's national sport, notably Rugby Union, which has been called "the new opium of the people". Rugby in Wales is something of a democracy, where the doctor scrums alongside the miner. In both north and south Wales, rugby has become the new social symbol, or identifier, of Welshness, and is one of the few, if not the only, social phenomena that unites all the people of Wales. A national ambition, which has echoed down the centuries, found expression in the Stereophonics' song of 1999, "as long as we beat the English, we don't care". A potent mixture of social history was used by Phil Bennett in a pre-match team talk before leading Wales out against England in 1977:

> "They've taken our coal, our water, our steel. They buy our homes and live in them for a fortnight every year. What have they given us? Absolutely nothing. We've been exploited, raped, controlled and punished by the English – and that's who you are playing this afternoon".[78]

Clearly, communalism does not always extend to those living across the border, and it is difficult to contend that the Welsh are always an empathetic and tolerant people! However, there is a significant tradition of commonality and mutuality among the people themselves. It has been challenged by the individualism of post-modern and pluralist worldviews. However, a social pattern and tradition of commonality, mutuality, and communitarianism, can be identified in its mutating forms.

To what extent a community reflects a legacy of *cymhortha, gwerin,* or socialism in Wales, will need to be evaluated. Contextualised mission in Wales must be responsive to it and to current changes, if it is to avoid appearing alien to the community it seeks to serve. Section Two will show how the *Approaches* succeeded in this, before 'good practice' for the future can be explored.

---

78 Phil Bennett, quoted in Rees, *Bred*, 151.

The Political Context of Wales

"Welsh History"[79]

We were a people taut for war; the hills
Were no harder, the thin grass
Clothed them more warmly than the coarse
Shirts our small bones.
We fought, and were always in retreat,
Like snow thawing upon the slopes
Of Mynydd Mawr; and yet the stranger
Never found our ultimate stand
In the thick woods, declaiming verse
To the sharp prompting of the harp.

Our kings died, or were slain
By the old treachery at the ford ...
We were a people bred on legends,
Warming our hands at the red past.
The great were ashamed of our loose rags ...
We were a people, and are so yet.
When we have finished quarrelling for crumbs
Under the table, or gnawing the bones
Of a dead culture, we will arise
And greet each other in a new dawn."

The geographical distinction produced by Offa's dyke, the otherness of language and culture, and the consequent awareness of a distinct *ethnie*, has for centuries produced a longing in Welsh people for political independence and freedom from English control. Wales had its boundaries and its social space, but it also aspired to be a distinct political entity, an independent nation.

Gerald of Wales (1146-1223) described how the Welsh were "passionately devoted to their freedom and to the defence of their country: for these they fight", and that "The English are striving for power, the Welsh for freedom ... The English, I say, want to drive the Welsh out of the island and to capture it for themselves".[80] He also quoted an individual, known as "the old man of Pencader", who said, famously:

---

79 Thomas, *Poems 1945-1990*, 36.
80 Gerald of Wales, *The Journey Through Wales and The Description of Wales* (London: Penguin, 2004), 233, 274.

"I do not think that on the Day of Direst Judgement any race other than the Welsh, or any other language, will give answer to the Supreme Judge of all for this small corner of the earth".[81]

This supposed prophecy, of a continuing Welsh identity and location, became a basis and inspiration for much medieval Welsh poetry, struggle and defiance in the face of a strengthening English threat.

There were brief periods of relative independence, if not security, in which leaders sought to lay the foundations of nationhood. The two parliaments of Owain Glyndŵr, in the Machynlleth area in 1404 and 1406, had followed the institutions of various rulers who governed some or most of Wales. They provided a point in history, or mythology, that later generations could look back to as a symbol of lost freedom. However, it was the death of Llewellyn, the last Prince of Wales, in 1282, that marked the end of independence.

Some thought that the prophet's hope had been realised when Henry Tudor, of Anglesey descent, won on Bosworth Field, to end the Wars of the Roses. Although Welshmen did well in Court for a season, it was not to last. Henry Tudor's son, Henry VIII, completed what Edward had begun in the Act of Union of 1535 and 1542.

(the) "dominion of Wales shall stand and continue for ever from henceforth incorporated united and annexed to and with his realm of England … minding and intending to reduce them to the perfect order notice knowledge of the laws of this realm and utterly to extirpate all and singular the sinister customs and usages differing".[82]

The Act sought the total elimination of Welsh laws, way of life, customs

---

81 Gerald of Wales, *Journey & Description*, 274.
82 J. Raithby, ed., *Statutes at Large of England and of Great Britain* (London: George Eyre and Andrew Strahan, 1811), 243-245, 407-408.

and language, and thus to destroy the Welsh identity. In the words of Humphreys, "Henry VIII was always a demanding lover. Too often his tender embrace could end in a kiss of death".[83] From the time of the Act of Union, the official policy of the State for "the dominion of Wales" was one of absorption.

These policies led many in Wales to an acceptance of Britishness, despite it being an extension of English identity. The desire to be anglicised, in order to succeed, resulted. Others felt like strangers, or second-class citizens, in their own country. The English were perceived as arrogant, patronising and superior, regarding the Welsh as quaint and rustic.[84] Regardless of the truth of the stereotypes, it was inevitable that some of the opprobrium would rub-off on the national psyche. Many have described features in Welsh people, including a sense of inferiority, a lack of entrepreneurship, servility, self-deprecation, passivity, low confidence, and as having "a bi-polar relationship with optimism".[85]

The Roots of Welsh Nationalism

The lack of political independence and self-government made the idea of a Welsh nation problematic, given its political subservience to England. The collective memory of English conquest and assimilation has shaped ideas of Welsh nationhood. According to R. S. Thomas, the poet, "... You cannot live in the present. At least not in Wales ...".

Political nationalism in Wales, developing largely in the twentieth century, was a reaction to internationalist socialism as well as British rule.

---

83 E. Humphreys, *Conversations and Reflections* (ed. M. W. Thomas; Cardiff: University of Wales Press, 2002), 110.
84 J. Glyn, "I Ba Raddau y mae Gwead 'Psyche' Hunaniaethol y Cymry yn Brawf o'u 'Coloneiddiad'?" (MA, Prifysgol Cymru Aberystwyth, 2006), 16; Davies, *History*, 66.
85 Williams, *When was Wales*, 113; Rees, *Bred*, 151.

The catalysts that turned an idea into a movement were the building of a military bombing school at Penyberth on the Llŷn Peninsula in 1936, and the drowning of the Tryweryn Valley in 1963.[86] In these flashpoints in Welsh-speaking areas, a military base was built, before being destroyed by arson, and the valley was flooded to provide water for Liverpool. In both cases, objections were widespread, but largely ignored, and so triggered a wider movement. The Nationalist Party, *Plaid Cymru,* and *Cymdeithas yr Iaith Gymraeg* came to prominence as a result.

By 2012 *Plaid Cymru* had one of the four Welsh seats in the European Parliament, three of the forty Welsh seats in the Westminster Parliament in 2015, and 206 of the 1264 local authority seats. In the 2011 National Assembly election, *Plaid Cymru* polled 19% of the popular vote. Some saw Welsh life as being re-invigorated by nationalism, however, this political nationalism was only one aspect of a wider cultural nationalism.

Civic Nationalism

Since the devolution settlement, and the establishing of a National Assembly in 1998, a new civic nationalism has grown, bringing its own self-confidence. The lack of civil institutions had been seen as a significant lack in Welsh nationhood, but, through the twentieth century, they were established in Wales in increasing number. They developed on an incremental basis from about 1870, based on the social and economic changes taking place at the time. They include the National Library, the National Museum, the Welsh universities, following Aberystwyth in 1893, the national anthem, the BBC's Welsh region, Cardiff being made the national capital, by London, in 1955, the Welsh Office in 1964, S4C in 1982,

---

86 E. Thomas, *Capel Celyn: Deng Mlynedd o Chwalu 1955-1965* (Llandybïe: Cyhoeddiadau Barddas a Chyngor Gwynedd, 1997), 6-14; Carter, *Against the Odds,* 24, 93.

the Welsh Medium Education and the Language Act, and the National Assembly building itself. These institutions, along with sporting, musical and artistic icons, and new law-making powers, represent a distinct national context that is decidedly distinct from England. The progress has been incremental but rapid. A new and confident Wales has emerged, that Carter describes as a "rising and revived Welshness".[87]

These developments have, however, not been the aspiration of every Welsh person. The vote to establish the National Assembly in 1997 was only won by the narrowest of margins. Nevertheless, as has also been traced, the rise in the popular vote in favour of nationalism, and the proliferation of national institutions, demonstrates a changing and increasingly confident nationally-minded context. Whether, or not, this leads to full political independence in the future, the degree of sympathy for nationalist aspiration in an area will be a significant factor in understanding the context.

Christian involvement in political activism, as an expression of mission, is contested in an increasingly secular and post-Christendom culture. The Church's prophetic voice may be more and more from the margins in British and Welsh Wales. However, Welsh nationalism was founded by people of Christian conviction, and leaders of *Plaid Cymru*, and *Cymdeithas yr Iaith Gymraeg* in the twenty-first century, have been Christians or people very sympathetic to Christian convictions. As with other aspects of the Welsh contexts, political activism in mission will depend on context.

Section Two will show how different *Approaches* adjusted to the rising awareness of Welsh identity, institutions, independence and government, and Section Three will suggest how effective calibration can be made, and new opportunities grasped.

---

87 Carter, *Against the Odds*, 145.

Section Two:

Approaches: How have the Churches been doing Mission?

We will now consider the state and strength of churches in Wales, and then see how they have been doing mission at the start of the third millennium. This will involve a detailed look at how six different *Approaches* to mission have developed, showing their effects on the churches as well as on the communities they serve. However, local church mission in Wales will need to produce numerical church growth, in the present and the future, if its mission is to be sustainable in the medium to long term. For some churches, such growth was a primary objective, but, for all, an increasing number of churches, leaders and members will be needed to instigate, sustain and extend their mission.

Welsh Nonconformity at the Start of the Twenty-first Century

The downward numerical trends for Welsh Nonconformity have been outlined in the previous section. The media have highlighted the decline, along with scholars in the fields of theology and sociology who speak of an end being in sight. Those involved in ministry in Wales, especially in the historic denominations, speak of an imminent *"anialwch ysbrydol"*,[88] a spiritual wilderness, and of disappearing denominations.[89] The land that was known as the Land of Revival has now been described as "faith's barren lands", and as having "given up on God".

Such a picture is difficult to gainsay, especially among the historic denominations. In the Presbyterian Church of Wales, historically the largest Nonconformist denomination, 1169 churches in 1982 had decreased to 885 in 1995, and to 680 in 2010.[90] In 2011, Brierley predicted 630 churches by 2015, but by January 2014, the number had already fallen to 599. 220 ministers, in 1982, had become 62 in 2010. Membership declined from 37,000 to 22,504 (-40%) over the same period.[91] By January 2014, there were 51 ministers, with a large proportion approaching retirement. In September 2013, the Moderator of the denomination bemoaned the fact that 50% of the churches were without pastoral oversight, a condition that has been shown to accelerate decline.

---

88 M. Ll. Davies, "Eglwys y Dyfodol," *Traethodydd* 160 (2005): 230.
89 S. Bell, "Eglwys y Dyfodol," *Traethodydd* 160 (2005): 234, 239.
90 P. Brierley and B. Evans, *Yr Argoelion yng Nghymru: Adroddiad o Gyfrifiad yr Eglwysi, 1982* (London: Marc Europe, 1982), 32-33; P. Brierley, *UK Church Statistics 2005-2015* (Tonbridge: ADBC, 2011), 10.1.
91 The denomination's own statistics are even more bleak, showing a 66% decrease over the period.

"Over half the churches within our denomination are without pastoral oversight, and most of our full-time ministers will reach retirement age during the next ten years. There are many churches with 10 or fewer members, resulting in an actual congregation of two or three, many of them sad and lifeless, overcome by the thought that they will be the last generation of worshippers in their area".[92]

The ageing demographic of the traditional denominations will lead to a rapidly accelerating decline in the next decade, as the last generation passes away. This will be exacerbated by the fact that many members rarely attend worship services, merely paying their membership fees to preserve a connection with the family's chapel, an icon of rural Welshness. The progressive reduction of those attending will draw the local church below the critical mass for its survival.

The Union of Welsh Independents, *yr Annibynwyr*, showed the same trends. 746 churches in 1982 had become 421 by 2012 (-44%), and 210 ministers had reduced to 76 (-64%), with a predicted decline to 382 churches with 54 ministers in 2015.[93] Methodist churches had declined similarly with 553 churches and 100 ministers in 1982, to 208 churches (-62%) and 58 ministers (-42%) in 2010, with membership falling from 17,600 to 9,025. The United Reformed churches were 163 in number in 1982, but down to 110 in 2010 (-33%), with membership down by 53%, between 1995 and 2010, to 2,696.

The Baptist Churches in Wales presented a more mixed picture. On the surface, a 20% decline in the number of congregations between 1995 and

---

92 T. Lewis, "Trefor's Challenge to Transform Tomorrow," *The Treasury* (September, 2013): 1.
93 Brierley and Evans, *Yr Argoelion yng Nghymru*, 36-37; Brierley, *Statistics 2005-2015*, 10.2.

2007 suggests the same pattern. However, there are two Baptist Unions in Wales: The Baptist Union of Wales (BUW), and the English language churches that belong to the Baptist Union of Great Britain (BUGB). The two Unions, together, had 833 churches in Wales with 311 ministers in 1982, which had reduced to 515 BUW churches and 177 BUGB churches in 1995. By 2010, the numbers had reduced further to 429 BUW churches (-17%) with 108 ministers, and 116 BUGBI churches (-35%) with 61 ministers. The proportion of ministers to churches, especially in the English language churches, was much higher than in the other denominations mentioned, reflecting a slower rate of decline, and, in some cases, clear evidence of growth. Welsh language churches, in contrast, experienced the same shrinkage and shortage of ministers as the other Welsh language denominational churches.

The English language Baptist churches have been affected by trends coming from outside of Wales. They had learnt from the growth of Independent Evangelical churches, Pentecostal churches, and those influenced or started as a result of the Charismatic Movement. The Independent Evangelical churches were responsible for the founding of new churches linked to various Evangelical networks. The Associating Evangelical Churches of Wales (AECW) had 56 churches in 1995, with 4,964 in attendance. In 2012, there were 57 churches, with 54 ministers and 2,893 members. Attendance was a higher figure than membership in the Evangelical churches, and the high proportion of ministers to churches may explain the absence of the decline trends seen in the older denominations. Other networks, based across the border in England, had a smaller number of Evangelical churches in Wales, but reflected the same patterns. The Fellowship of Independent Evangelical Churches (FIEC) had grown from 3 churches in 1995 to 25 in 2010, and the Evangelical

Fellowship of Congregational Churches from 3 churches to 7.[94] According to Brierley, there were a further 44 independent churches in 1995, that had increased to 48 by 2010. These developments in Welsh Nonconformity began, initially, in the early twentieth century, when groups left the denominational chapels following the revival of 1904/5. A second wave of secessions occurred in the second half of the century as a result of resistance to ecumenical trends, followed by a small number of new church plants in the twenty-first century.

The Independent Evangelical growth trends are paralleled by the growth of Pentecostalism in Wales, which also began subsequent to the religious revival of 1904. According to Brierley, the Apostolic Church had 19 churches in Wales in 1995, 37 in 2005, and 38 in 2010. The Assemblies of God had 73 churches in 1995 and 66 in 2010, although attendance had grown from 4,194 to 6,700 in the same period.[95] The Elim Pentecostal Church had 29 churches in 1995 and 36 in 2010, although attendance had declined from 2,729 to 2,650 in the same period. Brierley gives a total for Pentecostal churches of 163 churches, 248 ministers, and 13, 507 members in 2010. It is perhaps a significant indicator of trends that the number of Pentecostal ministers exceeds the combined total for the historic Nonconformist denominations of the Presbyterian, *Annibynwyr*, Methodist and URC churches.

Alongside with the second phase of the growth of Evangelical churches, the Charismatic movement in England began to influence and to start churches in Wales. From the 1980s, churches were begun on something of a franchise basis, by the Pioneer, New Frontiers, Ichthus, Ground Level, Ministries Without Borders, Multiply, Salt and Light, Covenant Ministries

---

94 Brierley, *Statistics 2005-2015*, 5.2, 5.3.
95 J. Gallacher, *Challenge to Change* (Swindon: BFBS, 1995), n.p.; Brierley, *Statistics 2005-2015*, 9.1.4.

and Vineyard networks. Together with other smaller groups and new churches, Brierley gives a total of 57 churches within these networks in 2010, with 85 leaders and 4,885 members. None of these networks, however, have any representation in Welsh language churches or communities. Their apparent Englishness, and the strong connections with their centres in England, would be considered alien in such communities. Other churches, of an ethnic minority or African Pentecostal nature, have been started in a similar way, from outside Wales, totalling 18 churches, 30 ministers and 1,722 members in 2010, largely in urban areas.[96]

The growth of the number of newer churches is a significant trend, which in many parts of Wales represents a renewal of a decaying Nonconformity. In comparison to the number of Nonconformist buildings scattered across Wales, they still represent a minority, but when the number of leaders, demographics, new congregations, and innovative expressions of mission are considered, they represent the growth edge. This chapter will seek to show whether their approach to mission, and any adjustments to the distinctives of Welsh contexts, account for their growing presence and influence.

In 1995, the authors of the latest comprehensive survey of Welsh churches spoke of a day when the number of new growing churches would exceed those closing:

> "The third trend is of a new generation of churches, from a variety of backgrounds and traditions, being planted since 1960. The numbers are small but the rate is increasing. ... As all of these trends are operating simultaneously, of interest is at what point the impact of decline will be overtaken by the impact of growth."[97]

---

96 Brierley, *Statistics 2005-2015*, 9.2.4-9.3.4, 11.2.1-6.
97 Gallacher, *Challenge*, chapter six.

It had not happened then, nor is it generally evident a decade into the twenty-first century. However, the growth trends described above suggest that the confidence expressed then is still valid, and that, after the fifteen intervening years, the evidence for effective and growing churches is clearer.

The *Waleswide* Survey of 2012

In 2011 and 2012 *Waleswide / Cymrugyfan* circulated a questionnaire to leaders of churches, seeking to find out the current nature and effectiveness of mission in Wales. With the cooperation of most of the denominational leaders, the Evangelical Alliance in Wales, and the Evangelical Movement of Wales, 588 Nonconformist ministers were identified, 386 responded to the questionnaire, and 283 did so fully. The findings of the Survey thus reflect the circumstances and views of approximately half of those ministering in Wales in the first decade of the twenty-first century, and represent the spectrum of Nonconformist denominations. (Chart 1, see Appendix.) The leaders of the new networks, together with English-speaking Baptists, reflect the shift in growth and strength from the historic Paedobaptist denominations (Presbyterian, *Annibynwyr*, Methodist and URC).

The questionnaire asked for details of growth and decline. Therefore, it is probable that those with a sense of progress or achievement would be more likely to complete the questionnaire, whereas leaders of declining churches might be less inclined to respond. The responses do not include the hundreds of churches without ministerial oversight. In the case of the Presbyterian Church of Wales, this meant that half their churches were not approached. This would indicate that decline in the historic denominations is greater than the figures suggest. Nevertheless, when these qualifications and limitations are taken into account, the information received from the questionnaire represents the fullest enquiry into the condition and mission of churches in Wales since the survey of 1995.

Growth and Decline Patterns

The attendance figures for 2010, compared to those of 2000, for the churches of the leaders responding, show that up to half these churches have grown numerically. This is a markedly different trend from that described previously, and may reflect the reluctance to respond in the cases of non-growth. Those churches which are growing are divided between those with marginal growth, and those which evidenced growth over the decade as well as in the single year of 2010. The criterion adopted is of at least five additions over the decade and two in the single year, the '5:2' churches, which gives some measure of any sustained effectiveness, at least in numerical terms (Chart 2).[98]

The additions recorded during the decade and the single year are divided between those who had professed faith in Christ from within a church community, the *internal converts*, and *external converts* who have been added from outside a church community. The data shows more growth from outside the churches than from within, which is an encouraging feature for hopes of future survival. However, the proportion being added to Welsh language churches is small, especially those coming from outside the church community. New additions to the worshipping community in Welsh language churches, for the most part, are internal, in that they were already members of the churches, but previously non-attending. The additions to bilingual churches are small for the 10% of respondents who identified themselves as such (Chart 3).

The additions, for the decade and the single year, show an uneven

---

98 The threshold was set low because so few churches were seeing any additions, and even fewer were experiencing growth greater than 5:2. The two figures were used to show additions over a period, rather than sudden bursts. Such additions, however, do not indicate growth overall, as some 5:2 churches lost more members through departures or death than their additions through people coming to faith and joining the church.

distribution when compared to the proportion of leaders from different denominations completing the Survey (Chart 4). The historic Paedobaptist denominations show lower growth, reflecting the number of Welsh language churches that attract additions from among their nominal membership. The Charismatic and Pentecostal churches recorded additions proportionately more for the number of churches represented. The nature of their mission, and the extent to which it adapted to the distinctives of the Welsh contexts, will be a significant pointer to effective mission in the future.

With 25% of the population of Wales living in the Cardiff and Newport areas, 24% in the Valleys, 22% in Swansea and the south-west, 7% in mid-Wales, 12% in the north-east and 10% in the north-west, the majority of the growth described has occurred in south Wales. However, the churches that are growing according to the 5:2 criterion, were found in the same proportion (40% of the churches) in urban, Valleys, or small town contexts. In contrast, only 20% of churches in rural areas met the criterion (Chart 5). However, this consistency was not found when considering the proportion of 5:2 churches in different regions (Chart 6).

How the Churches Communicated their Message

The questionnaire recorded how churches sought to communicate their message. For analysis purposes, the options were grouped into four categories: communication through church services of some kind,[99] through relationships and informal gatherings,[100] through direct evangelism in the community,[101] and through work with youth and

---

99 SERVICES includes Sunday preaching and Guest Services.
100 RELATIONAL includes Christianity Explored, Alpha and outreach meals.
101 DIRECT includes home visitation, literature distribution, street contact and preaching or sketch board.

children[102] (Chart 7). The responses show a continuing reliance on attractional methods, where a church building, and the services held in it, play a prominent role. Mission focussed on a church's building reflects an orientation that worked well in a Christendom context, but has been seen to be increasingly ineffective in a post-Christendom or secular context. That this emphasis was still seen as effective in some parts of Wales would suggest regional variations in degrees of secularisation. A significant number of churches regard preaching services in the church building as their primary approach to mission. It will be seen that such an approach has greater traction in rural and Welsh language areas, where chapel-going still has a place in community life, be it on Sundays, funerals or other social gatherings.

In the responses that recorded how people actually came to faith during the decade (Chart 8), it is not only the influence of church services that is evident, but also the greater proportion of people who came through personal relationships, evangelistic courses and events.[103] This shows some adjustment to the post-Christendom context. If, as revealed in the *Tearfund* 2007 research, 72% of the population of Wales are closed to further church involvement, whether they are de-churched or un-churched, these trends in mission are inevitable, and will increasingly become the norm.

How Churches Connect to their Communities

The leaders recorded the ways that the churches under their care were connected to their communities. For analysis purposes, the options are again grouped into categories: those that were related to the church's

---

102 YOUTH includes school assemblies, holiday clubs and youth outreach.
103 "Parents Following" records the number of adults who joined a church after their children had been involved.

existing provision for its own members,[104] the provision of a café open to the community,[105] those that were related to the needs of families,[106] the particular needs in the community,[107] youth provision,[108] or some kind of learning provision[109] (Chart 9). Respondents were asked to record activities that had been used over the decade, and the two activities that were used the most.

These groups of activities represent the mission of local churches as they interface with their communities. The fact that half the community connections were initially organised for the church communities themselves, and that half the churches had five or fewer connections, demonstrates that the churches' mission is focussed, at least initially, on its own people (Chart 10). The patterns reflect an inward looking, centripetal, mission, rather than an outward, centrifugal and missional orientation. This is exacerbated by the fact that churches without ministerial oversight, which might be even less well organised for such activities, are not included in this data.

The Survey also shows some correlation between the churches with more than seven links to their community, and those which are growing by the 5:2 criterion (Chart 11). The missiological approach of these churches, and the extent to which their approach adjusted to the nature of their community's particular Welshness, will give helpful pointers to effective

---

104 CHURCH RELATED includes activities for children, youth and the elderly, counselling and any use of the building.
105 Identified as CAFE RELATED.
106 FAMILY RELATED includes nursery provision, parenting courses, and marriage care.
107 NEED RELATED includes debt counselling, *Foodbank*, *Street Pastors* and help for the unemployed or prisoners.
108 YOUTH RELATED includes after-school clubs, school assemblies, sports training or teams.
109 LEARNING RELATED includes IT training, Literacy training, Welsh learning, and cultural activities.

mission in Wales in the twenty-first century.

Regional Variations in Expressions of Mission

How local churches expressed their mission varied in the different regions of Wales. The fact that the majority of the population is located in the cities and Valleys of the south means that most churches were located in these areas, and, therefore, that most local church mission is expressed there. When, however, the percentage use of approaches to mission is considered for each area, underlying trends are evident which are not distorted by the number of churches (Charts 12-15).

The north west region, where the Welsh language and traditional patterns of Welsh Nonconformity remained strongest, use fewer forms of Relational evangelism, and slightly more from the Direct activities group. The use of Services remains high, and because churches in the region have an older age profile, fewer forms of Youth outreach are used. In the south and Valleys, by contrast, all approaches are used, with slightly less reliance on Services and Direct activities. This latter trend may be explained by the greater community and social action involvement in the south and Valleys when compared with the north west region.

The connections that churches have with their communities, for social action (Charts 16-21), show lower levels of involvement in mid Wales and the north west. In these communities, traditional forms of church and mission, linked to the Welsh language, remain stronger. This is especially true in relation to Church, Café, Family and Need Related mission activities, and less so for Youth and Learning activities where patterns are more consistent. These variations will be seen to be significant when the responses of leaders, from each *Approach* to mission, are considered.

How the Six *Approaches* to Mission worked in Wales

Through its mission, the local church seeks to reach the community around it. Prior to the twentieth century it was largely evangelistic in nature, with social action as a consequence. However, as the new century developed, changes in the nature of mission followed significant theological changes in the churches of the West. The rise of theological Liberalism led to an increasing shift from an Evangelistic *Approach* to mission to one more concerned exclusively with the temporal welfare of people.

These two *Approaches*, Evangelistic and Liberal, represent two ends of a spectrum. Between them, four other *Approaches* can be identified. The Evangelistic *Approach* is best seen as including two *Approaches*, E1 and E2. The *Missio Dei Approach* represents an attempt to forge a middle way between the Evangelistic and Liberal ends of the mission spectrum. The Lausanne *Approach* is essentially Evangelistic, but has been significantly influenced by the *Missio Dei Approach*. The Emergent *Approach* seeks be an amalgam of the best elements of the other *Approaches*. In essence the elements in the spectrum can be described as follows:

- E1 churches see mission as proclamation only, and social engagement as a pastoral activity, at best, not a part of mission.

- E2 churches see social action as a bridge into the community around them, through which their message can be heard and gain credibility.

- Lausanne churches see evangelism and social action as equal partners in their mission.

- The Emergent *Approach* seeks to do mission inclusively,

incarnationally, informally by works, rather than by word.

- The *Missio Dei Approach* is an ecumenical initiative that sees mission as involvement in all aspects of God's world. Evangelism might be one aspect.

- Liberal churches see mission as exclusively concerned with social reform and relief.

Most of these *Approaches* would use the term "missional", referring to outward-looking, centrifugal, non-traditional forms of mission. The term was first used in the 1990s by the *Gospel and our Culture Network*, and notably by Guder.[110] Since then, the term "missional", or "mission-shaped", has been used widely by the different *Approaches* to contextualised mission. The exact meaning has varied according to the perspective of the one using it, and, as such, it is more an emphasis than an *Approach*.

---

110 D. L. Guder, ed., *Missional Church: A Vision for the Sending of the Church in North America* (Grand Rapids: Eerdmans, 1998), 1-17; Keller, *Center*, 251, 255.

Approaches to Mission

The Evangelistic Approach to Mission

In Wales, the efforts of Puritan, Nonconformist and later Methodist churches were primarily evangelistic in nature. Literacy work done through Griffith Jones' Circulating Schools was intended as a way to enable people to read the Bible and so come to, and grow in, personal faith. Mission and the evangelism of the individual were regarded as broadly synonymous terms. Churches were motivated by a desire to see the salvation of individuals, through Christ's coming into the world to reconcile sinful and alienated people to the holy and just God. The evangelistic imperative was such a priority that social action would not be put on a par with it. This *Approach* emphasised the proclamation of the message, with social concern and action a necessary consequence. However, as theological Liberalism developed a social gospel, Evangelistic churches tended to react and retreat into Pietism, so that their mission was solely evangelistic, and actually avoided social engagement.[111] This was a trend that tended to isolate churches from their surrounding communities, especially as society changed with the decline of Christendom. Following the religious revival of 1904/5, and the formation of Evangelical and Pentecostal mission halls separate from the main Nonconformist denominations, this trend was accentuated.

---

111 Pietism was a seventeenth century renewal movement that emphasised the inner spiritual life of the believer, and tended to neglect social and political action. Bebbington, *Evangelicalism*, 211-228.

What the Questionnaire and Interviews showed

Churches and leaders who practiced the Evangelistic as a heraldic approach to mission (E1) emphasised the priority of preaching the gospel, either orally or by literature. They did not give priority to social action, often associating it with the social gospel of theological Liberalism. One leader expressed the essence of this *Approach*:

> "We believe that broadly the biblically-mandated and time-honoured means of preaching, personal conversation, pastoral visitation, together with the consistent godly living of the membership, backed by prayer, are most likely to be honoured by the Sovereign Lord in a day of spiritual famine".

Their proclamation would normally be centred on the church building, usually in a Sunday service. Such methods reflect an attractional approach to mission, where people are invited to hear a message, and to respond to it personally. Such preaching might be supplemented by services or preaching in the open-air, street conversations of an evangelistic nature, or systematic home visitation, but without social action as a part of mission.

The E1 *Approach* often reflects underlying Calvinistic theological assumptions, where mission is driven by a conservativism based on biblical precedence, rather than activism or pragmatism:

> "It is also fair to say that our strong Calvinistic convictions lead us to believe that evangelism must begin in the prayer meeting, as regeneration is the work of God alone, and without it no one will repent and believe. Every conversion is a miracle ... We rejoice when we see conversions but we do not get anxious when a year or two goes by without a conversion, neither do we change our basic approach."

One leader saw all the evangelistic missions of the previous century as ineffective, being "the quick fix of unbiblical novelties". Another leader expressed a reluctance to be involved in community engagement in order to distinguish the present church from its theologically Liberal past. This E1 *Approach* continued practices that had been effective for generations, expecting that this would still be the case: "preaching the Old Time Gospel Message with none of the modern methods!" The tried and tested methods were "the pattern set down in Scripture, and that, as such, it is effective in every cultural context."

Such approaches to mission in E1 churches in Wales were strongly influenced by the teaching and example of Dr Martyn Lloyd-Jones, who became a minister in Port Talbot before moving to Westminster Chapel in London. Whilst in Port Talbot,[112] and later in Westminster,[113] he phased out the church's social programmes, concentrating on evangelistic preaching. He taught that it was the responsibility of the local church to save souls, for which religious revivals were a vital factor and need.[114] In these, and other aspects, his thinking was of "foundational importance to what was eventually to become the Evangelical Movement of Wales",[115] and widely formative for the missiological direction of E1 churches.

As contacts with the wider community became harder, however, some E1 leaders began to make adjustments within the *Approach*, seeking to make church services more accessible, but maintaining a mission approach that was attractional in nature. Community contact was a preparation for

---

112 Jones, "Lloyd-Jones and Wales," in Atherstone and Jones, *Engaging with Martyn Lloyd Jones*, 64; B. Bailie, "Lloyd-Jones and the Demise of Preaching," in Atherstone and Jones, *Engaging with Martyn Lloyd Jones*, 168.

113 J. Coffey, "Lloyd-Jones and the Protestant Past," in Atherstone and Jones, *Engaging with Martyn Lloyd Jones*, 322-323.

114 Randall, "Revival," in Atherstone and Jones, *Engaging with Martyn Lloyd Jones*, 91-113.

115 Jones, "Lloyd-Jones in Wales," in Atherstone and Jones, *Engaging with Martyn Lloyd Jones*, 73.

church attendance:

> "We are currently going through a period of change... The first stage of this change is to adapt our morning services so that they are more accessible to unchurched people and our own members/attenders have the confidence to invite people along. Alongside this we are looking to equip our members/ attenders to share their faith in their workplaces etc. because we are recognising that today to get the gospel out, we need to get out with the gospel".

In some cases, as above, there was a transition developing from mission centred on a Direct approach [home visitation, street contact and preaching, literature distribution and sketch board] to a more Relational one [courses such as *Alpha* or *Christianity Explored*, or a social event or meal with a speaker]. Others had found that attendance through responding to invitations from members had significantly diminished, whether for a normal Sunday or a special event.

However, such isolation did not seem to apply in all Welsh contexts. In some Welsh language areas, connections between chapel and community are still remarkably strong. In fact, the chapel is still seen as a cornerstone of the community. For one such church, there was no dis-connect, as the community still came to services in significant numbers. For them, it was the substance of the preaching, within its building, which was important for mission:

> "To reach this traditional situation we are seeking to ensure faithful preaching of the word on the Sundays in each part of the pastorate ... There is nothing particularly Welsh about this, but we are seeking to protect the Evangelical testimony through the medium of Welsh for a Welsh rural community."

When asked how the community would hear this message, the answer was unequivocally attractional:

> "They would need to come inside the Chapel, so there is the need to maintain those services. We have a permanence, in the sense of 10 o'clock and 6 o'clock Sunday evening, and people would be aware that there is a service going on in Chapel."

The continuing relevance of such an approach in a traditional Welsh community shows that secularism and post-Christendom realities have not yet affected all communities to the same extent. What has been effective for generations still has some relevance in some situations.

The second grouping of churches with an Evangelistic *Approach* to mission (E2) emphasised the proclamation of the gospel message, but were also intentionally engaged in social action. This social involvement was to be a support or bridge for the message, and to give a visual illustration of grace, which was thereby seen as well as heard:

> "... we have attempted to create opportunities to engage relationally with un-churched people who generally mistrust the church and are resistant to the gospel. In the light of this we have tried to communicate the gospel not only in word but through our actions e.g. community projects, kind deeds including debt advice and *foodbank* services and furniture recycling etc."

For these churches, the social action is done to support its message, and is not separate from it. One leader described the church's policy as, "We just look at community needs and position our evangelism around this opportunity." Some activities, such as *Foodbank*, night shelters for the homeless, unemployment clubs, or *Street Pastors*, might not have a verbal communication in them, but, nevertheless, the hope and reason for doing the activity was to commend a message that might be heard on another occasion, or the activity itself might provoke a question. E2 churches emphasised the importance of building relationships at a personal level as the essential precursor to hearing the message being offered.

"Everyone has come through relationships ...The clubs, social events, even Sunday Services, are not an end in themselves but lay foundations for relationships and friendships which must be experienced in everyday life to convince people you are genuine."

Despite the relative differences between E1 and E2 churches, they both make their message the priority. They both seek to do mission in their communities as the way to propagate their message. Churches described as E1 and E2 form a spectrum from those who resist any social engagement to those where mission always includes social action, with varying shades in between. There were E1 churches which were clearly opposed to social involvement, but others were merely continuing traditional chapel practices that had no place for it in a local church's mission. There were other E1 churches which provided nurseries, marriage care, care for the elderly, hospital and prison visiting, children and youth clubs, but saw these as relating to pastoral care or as a church activity, rather than mission. Mission in such churches is solely related to heraldic evangelism, and quite separate from social involvement. The questionnaire, therefore, showed E1 churches doing some of these activities, though E2 churches did them intentionally for mission.

The Evangelistic Message and Means of Communication

The Questionnaire did not ask leaders to state their primary message, but those doing interviews did so. Those with an Evangelistic *Approach* to mission, whether E1 or E2, prioritised the work of Christ, human need, and the benefits of a personal salvation:

- "Jesus Christ and him crucified... that people are sinful, that Jesus died as a substitute that we might be forgiven, and that faith brings forgiveness from God and the blessings of the gospel, new life, the hope of eternity".

- "The gospel, it begins with the righteousness of God who will punish sin. Salvation through the death and resurrection of Jesus".

- "The gospel. Christ Jesus came into the world to save sinners and calls people to repent and believe. It's the good news".

- "The biblical gospel. That would mean a God who saves sinners through Christ on the cross, atonement, makes them his children, by grace through faith".

- "It's got to be the gospel, however you package it. That's what we are about. Life change, new hope, however you slant it, that's what we are about. Grace, unmerited favour. You can come and meet with this Jesus who can change your life."

- "The gospel is the fact that Christ the Saviour came to earth to save us from our sins, that we might live life in all of its fullness and live in eternity with him forever. As the Westminster confession says, the chief aim of man is to glorify God and to enjoy him forever".

The only marginal difference was that E2 leaders gave additional emphasis to the resulting experience:

- "The primary message would be how does a man or a woman come into right standing with God. That would be the driver... That would motivate us. The answer would be to turn away from their sins, to repent of their life that they have lived, and to trust completely and wholeheartedly in the sacrificial death of Christ on the cross on their behalf..."

- "That through Jesus Christ they can have forgiveness of sins and, be part of his community, his family that he is building across the world ...we would also emphasise community a lot".

- "Our primary message is very simple, Jesus is Lord. What we seek to do as a church is to present the fact that Jesus is Lord... We help people to understand that God wants to fill every part of our lives and every part of our lifestyle with him as Lord".

- "The church's primary message is gospel based... to develop a deep relationship with God and to make a living commitment to him. Also encouraging them to look to him for their daily needs really".

- "That Jesus is the only one who can save, change and transform lives and communities. Jesus is the message of the church. All they bang on about is Jesus!"

Clearly, such a message of forgiveness, change, and hope is seeking to draw individuals into a personal relationship with Christ, and be involved in church and Christian service as a consequence. The emphasis on individual salvation did lead to a mission that looked to add people to the church and its mission, with some success.

The questionnaire also asked leaders to confirm how their church or churches sought to communicate their message through identifying the methods used, and the two "most used". They were also asked through what means people had actually come to faith and been added to the church. When grouped into the categories explained earlier (Pages 66 and 67), there were small yet significant differences between E1 and E2 (Charts 22 and 23). Both *Approaches* used church services to convey their message as one of their "most used" activities, but E2 churches tended to use both Sunday services and guest services more. E1 churches made greater use of Direct approaches to mission, whereas E2 had a greater use of Relational approaches, sometimes with two methods in the group used.

When asked by what means people had actually come to faith (Charts 24-25), the picture was more varied, but the patterns were the same. E1 churches saw the greatest number of people coming to faith through preaching, their priority approach. E2 churches, however, saw the greatest number coming through relational contact, and more people coming through all the other categories. It is noteworthy that even in the areas emphasised by E1 churches, such as preaching, visitation, and mission weeks, fewer churches saw people added through these means than in E2 mission of the same type. Less than 10% of E1 or E2 churches saw people added through mission weeks. These patterns would suggest that E1 churches were persisting with less effective approaches, and that E2's extra connections with the community made the evangelistic methods they adopted more effective.

When compared to the other *Approaches* to mission, the Evangelistic *Approaches* showed a marginally higher use of Services and Relational activities (Charts 32 & 34), whereas the use of Direct and Youth approaches was not dissimilar (Charts 35 & 37). The use of Youth methods was relatively consistent in all *Approaches*.

When considering the use of Services and Relational methods by Evangelistic churches, it was the 5:2 churches which made the greatest use of them (Chart 26). This greater use is one explanation for why certain churches grew more. The differences were marginal, but, with other factors yet to be considered, they begin to explain why the mission of some Evangelistic churches was more effective, in terms of numerical additions, than others. Churches with an E1 and E2 *Approach* had a proportionately greater number of 5:2 churches than other *Approaches* (Charts 27 & 28). This is but one measure of the effectiveness of the mission of the local church, but in terms of the future survival of Welsh Nonconformity it is not insignificant.

However, what is also a significant pointer to effective mission, is the difference between E1 and E2 churches, and their influence on their communities. The percentage of 5:2 churches was lower in E1 than E2. E1 churches relied on traditional methods of mission, whereas E2 churches had more connections with communities, and were connected more intentionally. Also, where traditional approaches were strongest, in north-west and mid Wales, the regional proportion of 5:2 churches was lower (Chart 29). Charts 30 and 31 show clearly the greater intentionality of E2 churches, particularly when some connections were, primarily, for church members.

Compared to other *Approaches* the charts comparing how churches were connected to their communities (Charts 39 to 45), show that Evangelistic churches have a lower level of engagement. This reflects the large number of E1 churches which did not have extensive connections, beyond church services and youth and children's work. Chart 39 shows that some Evangelistic churches did not see their building as part of a mission to serve the community through social action. This is in contrast to the 100% of such churches that saw their building as a means to communicate their message (Chart 32). Charts 41 and 43 reflect the same decision of many E1 churches not to engage in social action. Charts 42 and 44 reflect the pastoral emphases in E1 churches in work among children and youth, to which children in the community were welcome. Chart 45 shows a measure of disinclination to be involved in Learning Related mission. This will be considered further when contrasting it with the much greater emphasis of a Liberal *Approach* to mission.

Within both E1 and E2 churches, there were Charismatic and Pentecostal churches, often linked to *New Wine Cymru* network, which emphasise the place of the supernatural and miraculous in mission. This emphasis sees the miraculous, be it a healing, a vocal word of prophecy, special wisdom or knowledge, as a way to gain the attention of the hearer and give credibility to the message being spoken. Pentecostal missions give such a specific emphasis. Leaders were clear in this expectation:

> "Praying directly for needs then sharing the Gospel when prayer is answered. Welsh people in the valley communities soon start talking when things are happening!"

E2 churches, with the same emphasis and expectation of miraculous elements, would see such incidents as parallel and complementing social action. Both aspects would be seen as giving credibility to their message. The Survey did not collect data to support the effectiveness, or otherwise, of this aspect of the mission of Evangelistic churches, though anecdotal evidence was given in the questionnaire and the interview responses. There was, however, no widespread evidence of this emphasis leading to growth in the churches, or widespread influence on communities, in the responses that were given. The emphasis was not a part of church life or mission in traditional churches, but was evident in some growing Charismatic churches. The implications for mission of this emphasis will be considered in Section Three.

Adjusting to the Religious Aspects of Welsh Context

When asked in the *Waleswide* 2012 Survey about the religious context of their community, and their adjustment to it, the responses of Evangelistic churches fell into four categories.

Firstly, there were those who saw little current evidence of a distinct Welsh religious tradition, because decline of the chapels had occurred to such an extent that the majority of the population were oblivious to it. Regionally, such responses were in the urban and anglicised areas of south Wales, or in the east, close to the English border. What had been a common experience, had become merely a memory:

> "Many older people in the community have had some contact with the work and life of the church at some point in the past ... That context has changed and many of the young people we meet have little knowledge of real Christianity and see the church as irrelevant to them."

As a consequence, leaders in these areas, or who perceive their areas in this way, see no distinctiveness in the religious context of mission.

Secondly, there were those who recognised the negative legacy of Welsh Nonconformity, so that they felt mission had to be distanced from it. One church held events, deliberately, on a day other than Sunday, to mark a complete distinction from past traditions. However, memories, of what was regarded as an oppressive, boring and out-of-date chapel culture, could still be handed down to succeeding generations, and therefore remained a hindrance to generations which had themselves never attended chapel on a regular basis:

> "I believe these folk have rejected what they have experienced as Church... not Christ. The younger generations have little or no knowledge of Jesus and only imbibed the opinion of their elders that Church is boring."

The practice of adults sending their children to Sunday School still survived in certain places, but this sent an equally negative message to the younger generations:

"It paints a very morbid picture of Christianity... incredibly legalistic, and incredibly moralistic, and incredibly boring place to go... If you want your children moral send them to Sunday school, but, 'Why don't you go Mam?' 'Well, I've done my time in church, now it's your turn."

The chapels had an association with the past, and so were perceived as looking back not forward. This was seen as "living off yesterday's manna, and it is so stale now that you're actually getting sick from it." The chapel buildings, and the graves around them, were sending powerful messages of decline and deadness.

However, the chapel tradition was not just hindering mission in the wider community. It was seen as an active influence, hindering mission among those still attending a place of worship. This was, in part, due to the age of the remaining members, and the different needs and interests of the younger target audience. One denominational leader described the issues:

"We have a small elderly membership ... (name of place) is a holiday resort with a skewed elderly population and the church/chapel-goers among them are at the top end of that! ... We have a population to whom religion is a part of their culture ... We are trying to use the open door that it offers, but get rid of the cultural trappings that go along with it."

This description shows the challenges faced in transitioning approaches to mission in a traditional Welsh chapel context. However, the awareness shown of the opportunities as well as the difficulties, and the desire to innovate, is not always evident in such circles.

For some, the negative chapel legacy was an issue of theology as well as tradition. The chapels engendered a culture of respectability and self-righteousness, which, to leaders of Evangelical convictions, could create a barrier to their message of God's free acceptance by grace through faith: "People have a 'religious' default setting, so struggle with grace." In Welsh-speaking chapels, the charge was, "The Chapel used to uphold the culture and not the gospel." Now that secular bodies were shaping the cultural agenda, the chapels had lost even this role within society, and were left bereft of any strongly held gospel tradition.

Thirdly, there were those who saw the religious heritage of Welsh Nonconformity as still relevant to sections of the community, mostly the elderly. They saw this chapel legacy as an opportunity, not a hindrance, as many in their community were accepting of the church, without committing to it. Having some family still in the chapel was a link for mission, as "Everyone had a mum, dad or grandparent that went to church." Others saw clear opportunities for mission to the older generation through organising events responding to the national love of hymns with their associated tunes. They would also send preachers to local chapels to reach those still attending. One leader spoke of "a residual respectability about 'chapel-going' which means that over a third of our evening attenders are unbelievers". For them, an attractional approach, that used the chapel building, was still an opportunity for mission.

> "In a fairly traditional community, traditional methods work better than one might expect. People coming to church often expect and appreciate a building that looks and feels like a church."

This illustrates the lingering, and even pervasive, legacy of Welsh Nonconformity in some areas, where a lingering respect for God, chapel and ministers remained. The pattern was not uniform, but graded to different degrees in different areas. However, the diminishing influence on younger generations was testified to in all areas. For these, a different approach was needed. For them, one-to-one evangelism outside the church building, and outside of church meetings, was essential, which was "not pre-evangelism, nor general community involvement. It is deliberate, intentional, regular gospel conversations that take place in homes, shops and even a mosque".

Fourthly, there were those who saw the historic patterns of Welsh Nonconformity, in terms of loyalty to a chapel culture, preaching and even membership, as still influential in the whole community. These responses reflected the surviving legacy of Wales as a Nonconformist nation. They were expressed most strongly in Welsh-speaking rural areas. Here, where stable communities maintained patterns of work and culture, the chapel was still accepted as an integral part of the community alongside agriculture, *eisteddfodau*, choirs and village organisations, such as *Merched y Wawr*:

> "There is a suspicion of anything new and 'foreign' in nature - even contemporary worship - seeing 'new' things as 'temporary' - fashion can be made without it. An attachment to the society '*Pethe*' - a home, a chapel, learning and culture are much safer in this thinking."

These four attitudes to the strength of Welsh Nonconformity's religious legacy tended to be regional. In the cities and closer to the English border, with high levels of Anglicisation of language and culture, the influence was least. In the post-industrial Valleys, the negative legacy was strongest, whereas in rural areas the influence was still strong, albeit mostly in the older generations. In some stable Welsh language communities, the legacy was still perceived as a positive one in the wider community as well as the church. Mission, in these different contexts, has to adjust accordingly.

The Evangelistic *Approaches* to mission showed an awareness of this lack of uniformity, and those involved adjusted their mission to their immediate context. Those who minimised the religious legacy were in highly anglicised or secularised communities. Those who sought to take advantage of the chapel legacy saw it as a passing opportunity in the older generations. Those who saw the chapels' ongoing acceptance in their community, however, may have been belated exceptions. The general decline of chapels and membership would not encourage such confidence in the present or the future. However, whatever the response to the religious context, those with an Evangelistic *Approach* were deliberate and intentional in their adjustment to context because of their overarching belief in the importance and relevance of the message they were seeking to herald.

Adjusting to the Geographic Aspects of Welsh Context

As in the case of religious context, the influence of the geographic factors varied from region to region. In the communities bordering England, the highly anglicised cities and the coastal areas of south Wales, many communities were indistinguishable from communities across the border. The contextualisation of churches in these areas reflected these realities. One leader referred to the historic uncertainty of identity in the former county of Monmouthshire as a cause of a lack of a distinctive Welshness and an influence on their approach to mission:

> "I don't think our approaches to outreach are any different to any English area. At various times most of our area has been in England, but now in Wales due to boundary changes. We have a great Church tradition and heritage but it is not particularly Welsh."

In fact, something of an indifference to Welshness was expressed in response to the questionnaire. A border localism would seem to be set against any sense of national identity:

"As a border county this (i.e. Welshness) is not a particular issue. People's prime concern is very local identity rather than national identity."

Models and approaches to mission that are current and effective across the border, would be considered for use without question.

In marked contrast to these areas, the post-industrial Valleys, though situated adjacent to the most anglicised areas, had a distinct geographical identity because of the shape of the land. The steep valley sides had produced linear settlements, in rows of adjacent villages. These represent a distinct identity in the post-industrial Valleys, "Valleys Welsh".

"Many people here would see themselves as a 'valley person'. Their identity would be wrapped up in this, and to be a valley person is to be Welsh. The Welsh language is not widely spoken, and this valley identity seems to have taken its place."

The Evangelistic churches sought to respond to this, by identifying with their particular community within the valley, and by working with the strong social networks that existed. Leaders spoke of the breakdown of this social cohesion after the closure of the mines, and because people had to travel farther down the valley to find work. However, the tradition, and an expectation of it, still remained. The church's mission was adjusted to it:

"Friendship. Servanthood to locality through contacts, knowing needs. Close community & social consciousness... Church as local people involved with people in the community. Identity with families. Church integrated and involved and known".

In this way, mission demonstrated an engagement with the distinct localisms, resulting from social and economic factors, in the community that the churches were a part of. The distinctive nature of Valley communities also called for indigenous leaders, living in the community, understanding and identifying with it. The specific localism needed a specific response, each village being a distinct community that viewed itself as different and distinct from others, however close.

Rural communities and churches, isolated by mountains and poor lines of communication, retained similar local traditions and distinct Welsh identity. These conditions, in terms of the effects of isolation, were true in rural Denbighshire and Gwynedd. Leaders in rural Wales described their communities and their response:

> "In this community, being a family, and an extended family, is important. There is an identity, a historical identity, that is quite profound in the sense that this is Wales, this is where we belong. It is an ethnicity link to land, that is true of our situation here in a farming community."

In some cases, this connection to the land went back hundreds of years. As a result, church tradition and expressions of mission, had long pedigrees, and change was a prolonged process. The localism provided a detailed knowledge of people, families, and loyalties in the community, so mission could not be "hit and run".

The geographical rootedness seen in these rural situations represented the essence of a particular localism that had been reproduced in various forms where internal migration had taken people to Valley or urban situations. Here, loyalty to place, together with a certain insularity, found new expression. In rural Pembrokeshire, "Little England beyond Wales", the county identity was paramount.

> "People are Pembrokeshire, their identity is very much in the county. Perhaps in Pembrokeshire you wouldn't use the idea of Welshness in quite the same way. ... A Pembrokeshire mind-set is expressed in the Pembrokeshire phrases,

and their ways and manners, and also a very parochial way of looking at life with nothing happening outside of Haverfordwest."

A similar pattern was evident in the urban, and once industrialised, areas of Carmarthenshire.

"Llanelli is terribly parochial and 'one eyed' to the degree that I often think being Llanelli is more important than an overall Welsh identity. In this, it is the Town with the little village mentality."

The distinct local identity meant that programmes and evangelistic courses that worked elsewhere were less effective in Llanelli. Instead, local conversational involvement was seen as fruitful. One leader, in a very deprived part of the town, said that mission had to be deeply incarnational: "the community's question is not so much 'is it true?'. What they want to know is 'does it work?' - and more specifically 'does it work HERE?'" These responses to the local characteristics of the people show the awareness of those with an Evangelistic *Approach* to mission. Concern to communicate the message made appropriate connection with the people a high priority.

Another leader in Llanelli spoke of a reluctance among the people to travel beyond the locality: "to cross the Loughor is like going to Canada, crossing the Severn Bridge!" For them, mission in Llanelli sought to encourage a widening from what was local and small, encouraging a sense of ambition and self-belief:

"The robbery of poverty, which robs you of confidence, adventure, hope and ambition ... which is to do with Welsh village stump mentality. It is a rootedness and an identity with Wales in my village. It's like a tree that can only stretch so far with its roots in, it isn't going any further."

Their mission in the town, including a café with an art gallery, was done with a sense of excellence in order to cultivate a sense of civic pride. This adjustment to the needs of the locality showed the desire of those with an E2 *Approach* to mission to respond to the particular needs of the people in order to build the bridges over which their message may cross.

Adjusting to the Ethnic Aspects of Welsh Context

A Welsh ethnicity, whether perceived or inherited, was derived directly from a sense of place, and of being the people of that place. Where family descent had been connected with a particular locality for hundreds of years, the sense of distinct ethnicity was considered to be more than merely imagined.

> "There is a difference in the blood, in the constitution of the people. They're Celtic not Saxon. They have a different way of responding to things."

This awareness of difference had been intensified as well as diluted by inward migration. For the original inhabitants, the in-comers had heightened their sense of difference, whereas in the population as a whole, the original distinctives of the Welsh *ethnie* had been diminished. In rural communities, the original inhabitants and the in-comers would often remain substantially separate communities. In Welsh language areas, the two communities could exist side by side, but would rarely integrate. As a result, there was a suspicion of, and resistance to, Englishness, similar to that expressed in the post-industrial Valleys.

Where immigration had been high in an area for generations, as in Wales's larger towns and cities, approaches adopted from outside Wales, or leaders moving into Wales, would raise few objections. This was particularly true in the New and Charismatic churches, where patterns of mission, and even church affiliations, were of English origin. Such leaders often saw no difference in the local people from other parts of the United Kingdom. Leaders saw little evidence of Welsh ethnic distinctiveness:

> "We are a bit of an English enclave in a city close to the border so do not have a Welsh distinctive. Many of the present congregation moved into Wales with work e.g. relocation of government offices. But we do have a Welsh name."

Other leaders spoke in the same way, highlighting international influences within the church, not Welsh ones:

> "I don't think it is distinctly Welsh. We are English speaking and have no translation into either Welsh or Urdu! We live and reflect the ethnic mix of our wider community."

In Bangor, a university and hospital town with many international students and professionals, churches tried to respond to many nationalities. In Cardiff, the ethnic diversity, in terms of the church's mission, was decidedly varied:

> "We have an Eritrean congregation, South African congregation and youth congregation, which we believe reflects the modern day make-up of the City. ... We are thinking of starting a Welsh-speaking congregation."

Clearly, mission in such contexts was being directed to a very cosmopolitan society.

In the post-industrial Valleys, where inward migration has been negligible for half a century, mission was tailored to the community, indigenous leadership was seen as helpful, and imported approaches as alien:

> "The valley community is quite diverse - Alpha has not been particularly helpful though we have run two courses - Nicky Gumble is not very 'Valley Friendly' though the elderly quite like him. 'Table Talk' has been more useful

starting at a level much further back in people's understanding..."

The emotional legacies of decline, neglect and a perceived inferiority were also factors affecting mission to the deprived communities. There was what has been described as a "painful pessimism" where "the whole world is against us". Outward migration was seen as the only way to employment and self-improvement, and there was a pessimism that inward investment would be either short-term or unlikely. Unemployment was generational, so an 'us-and-them' attitude existed, especially against the English.

"We despise the English because we're defeated men and women, we were colonised. We do what the English tell us to do. They control your future. We don't hold our own future in our hands, in a way our future is dictated to us ... We just don't have the people who know anything other than the benefit culture, pessimism, depression, lurching from one crisis to the next and feeling this is a vicious circle that will never be broken."

This was described as a form of racism.

"Hating the English. Rugby. Drinking, hard drinking. Hating the English is the primary, I hate the ******* English is something that is terribly true... There is a real fear of outsiders, ignorance essentially. It borders on racialism, dangerous racism. It is not just anti-English it is people from ethnic backgrounds, Polish people. There is a real antagonism to people not from across the road..."

In Llanelli, people defined themselves in milder terms, as not being English: "It's not particularly anti-English but it is clearly proud that it is not English. It's a classic case of 'little brother' syndrome." However, the xenophobic hostility was encountered by those moving into Welsh-speaking rural areas, and one leader from southern Africa drew a striking comparison: "They feel threatened ... and are protective, similar to

Afrikaners."

However, when those from within the indigenous communities were describing these issue they saw things very differently:

"We don't like to brag ... we are quite self-effacing in that sense. We don't like egos... Probably arrogance is seen as something not to be tolerated in the community. Arrogance is English. ... Even in our language we use the passive tense more so than an assertive tense. We are very suspicious of those who are aggressively positive."

Those who contrast the indigenous *ethnie* with the in-comers, see the Welsh as humble, and as having an inferiority complex:

"... the opposite of the English public schoolboy Anglican. Everything I associate with that, you know, very confident, a bit brash, and arrogant sometimes. I'm not saying they all are. Welsh people tend to be the opposite... a reaction against the kind of inferiority complex, and not wanting to be like those English people. We are quite proud of being different from that kind."

The implication for mission in these communities was that methods and personnel needed to be indigenous. Where a church's mission was being organised, planned and delivered by non-Welsh people, great care was needed to respect local sensitivities. A leader in west Wales, originally from England, gave a blunt critique of the local people. They were described as emotional, friendly only on the surface, expressing willingness but not delivering, shy, quiet and withdrawn, and lacking commitment and perseverance. One might wonder whether a personality clash had been caused by the leader, who spoke of people having a real battle to get over hurt, and a tendency "to withdraw and go inside rather than take revenge." A clash of expectations, temperaments and even ethnicity was clearly evident. In this case, mission was struggling to adjust to local characteristics. The various tensions described illustrate how an awareness of ethnic differences could help or hinder Evangelistic mission.

Adjusting to the Linguistic and Cultural Aspects of Welsh Context

The regional variations seen in the geographical and ethnic factors were clearly paralleled in the linguistic and cultural characteristics. Historically, it had been the Welsh language that had been a bulwark in preserving and nurturing most ethnic and cultural distinctives. The Evangelistic *Approach* to mission had responded to Welsh language and culture in a spectrum of ways, from active support to conscious avoidance.

Firstly, there were the monoglot Welsh language churches which sought to do mission solely within Welsh-speaking communities, or to serve Welsh speakers in English language areas. The Evangelical Movement of Wales had encouraged the forming of new Welsh-speaking churches, separate from those that were English-speaking, in most regions of Wales. The issue of mono-lingual churches will be considered in the next Section, but a principle criticism will be mentioned here:

> "Too great an emphasis is placed on the language by many Welsh language churches, that they disregard their commission to reach out to all people."

The concern was that the Evangelistic message was being directed to Welsh speakers only, in areas where English speakers also lived. Such a charge, however, was not wholly accurate, as some churches provided simultaneous translation into English, and some held occasional English or bilingual services or events for English speakers who were learning Welsh. One respondent addressed the criticism directly:

> "What we have been offering to the community - Sunday services, Bible study, Sunday school has been primarily Welsh yet we do now offer bilingual

services and are open to change. The language should not be a hindrance but a help to the work which is to reach people for Christ."

Their Evangelistic mission, however, was inevitably to the Welsh-speaking community. This was expressed through involvement in Welsh language community events, such as choirs, charities, and through work with students, schools, or Welsh learners. In all cases, but one, Welsh language churches had retained the traditional chapel model, which was essentially attractional, with little deliberate mission into their community.

Secondly, there were bilingual churches which sought to reach and serve the two language communities. Some of these churches were largely English-speaking, yet sought to reach and serve the Welsh language community by running special events or services for Welsh speakers or Welsh learners. In these churches, there was a recognition that Welsh speakers often lacked confidence in speaking English, or had a strong preference for speaking and hearing Welsh. Consequently, the welcome, worship, prayers, and sometimes the sermon would be bilingual. In other churches, the morning service would be in English and the evening in Welsh, with simultaneous translation. In other churches, there was a monthly, or irregular, Welsh service. Children's work might have more Welsh language elements because most children in Welsh language areas would be in Welsh medium schools. Publicity and events would also be in both languages.

"... we have sought to be bilingual in all our activities... In mission with individuals we seek to use their heart language as much as is possible - this would include, where possible, the use of literature in the heart language. ... Finally, in recognition of the very large number of people locally who are Welsh Learners, we have begun a weekly Conversation Group for Welsh

Learners."

In one rural town in a Welsh language area, a separate church was started because an existing Evangelical church did not hold any services or mission through the medium of Welsh. The newer church did services in English on Sunday morning, and Welsh, with simultaneous translation, in the evening. They arranged all other events and connections to the community bilingually.

Thirdly, there were churches which nominally acknowledged the Welsh language. They would include Welsh in their services, with Welsh hymns, and in their events, with Welsh text in their publicity. This was described as an attempt to incorporate a Welsh flavour into church life and mission:

"Our churches are part of traditional village life. We use the language in some of our services. Our approach to evangelism and worship is distinctly 'Welsh' in ethos."

English language churches in Welsh language areas were seeking to use the language as a bridge to attract the majority population outside their walls. They retained English as the church's language, either out of a conviction that they had been led to do so; or because "English is not a bar to hearing the gospel;" or because "... we would function with no adverse results if 'Welsh' recognition disappeared." It was recognised, however, that:

"The language of the local clubs and chapels is Welsh. To be Welsh-speaking in this area is a considerable advantage particularly in relation to involvement in the community."

In terms of contextual mission, such a policy would seem to be impeding mission to a community where most people live through the medium of Welsh. It might be that the majority population feel somewhat excluded by the church's language policy, in the same way that English speakers in one area were said to be excluded by a Welsh-only provision.

In two churches, in predominantly English language areas, Welsh language connections were found to be a fruitful sphere for mission. They found that a high percentage of the community spoke some Welsh, or were learning, or had children in Welsh medium education. Running Welsh classes, a Welsh Learners Carol Service each year, a St David's event "with culture, cawl and the gospel" had become an annual community event.

Fourthly, there were churches that avoided the Welsh language, seeing it as either irrelevant or unhelpful. These views were expressed almost exclusively in anglicised border areas and cities, or in the post-industrial Valleys. In the Valleys, a hostility to the English to the east was matched by an equal animosity to the Welsh language to the west. The feeling that Welsh speakers saw them as in some ways less Welsh had engendered a hatred of the language. The Valleys spoke "English and bad language! There are a few Welsh speakers but they are few and far between." Another Valleys leader saw the Welsh language as merely "a conduit for language/culture", preferring a more relevant and contemporary image. Elsewhere, Welsh was seen as divisive, "a problem", a "hot potato", or simply irrelevant to the area. In such communities, appearing to promote a particular form of Welshness associated with the language, or the language itself, would be a hindrance to mission, in the same way that its absence would be farther west.

Except in areas like those just described, cultural features, festivals and icons were seen as opportunities for mission. Events linked to St David's Day, *Santes Dwynwen*, rugby games, or choral singing, especially hymn singing, were found to be good opportunities to connect with the wider community. Mission was felt to be more effective when it was "distinctly 'Welsh' in ethos."

Mission in Wales has to be sensitive to the prevailing cultural and language patterns of the particular community. The same attitudes and approach that would be helpful in one area would be counter-productive and alienating in another. English and Englishness would be seen as progressive and contemporary to some, or alien and threatening to others. The Welsh language and its associated culture would be seen as archaic or alienating to some, and patriotic and inclusive to others. Evangelistic churches showed sensitivity to language and culture in a nuanced response to the prevailing mores and preferences of their local communities. The exception would be the adoption of English as the language of church and mission in Welsh language areas.

Adjusting to the Social Aspects of Welsh Context

The influence of Wales' topography on social patterns has already been considered. Wales, as a "land of villages", has small linear communities in the Valleys, isolated rural settlements, and even village identities within urban areas. These small communities define social patterns, and have led to a tradition of close-knit, mutually supportive social networks, inter-connected by extended families.

> "In our community everyone knows everyone else! We have close knit communities who, through long tradition, support each other and this is vital to our communication with those in need."

In these communities, everyone is said to know everyone else, and the integration of outsiders can be a generational process. The interconnectedness is an opportunity for a church's mission to be an active part of the community, but the exclusivity can be a hindrance.

> "I think the local context is that there are tighter family groups making it

difficult for someone outside to 'break in'. ... The focus is on the immediate family and therefore, they are not readily outward looking."

The weakening of these communities, because of outward migration for work or inward migration of people without relational or family connections, has reduced these patterns, but they continue to be influential:

"Village community ... is so pretty personal. ... People are quite ready to converse & family life though not as strong as it was, in our community is not bad ... Also, village community so Church is fairly known & therefore trusted. ... Village/valley communities although not as were, the people are still personable/engaging/talkative/nosey which is still useful for the Church to utilise."

This response identifies the opportunity for mission in such communities. It is in these situations, especially in areas of social need, that the local church has found a servant role, which the community, in some cases, has come to expect:

"Through the commitment to serve in our coffee shop, we have been able to engage with the community and discover issues that arise, offer ourselves as a bridge to develop friendships ... (everyone seems to know each other's business). The community, on the whole, likes this kind of neighbourhood... The village population seem to require this type of knowledge and understanding from us."

Clearly, churches that are not involved in such social opportunities will have difficulty connecting to their communities. The patterns found in the community had also found their way back into the church, so that there was less of a cultural barrier between the two:

"We want to be relaxed, informal - come as you are church. We try to create the same 'let's have a cuppa' welcome you would get in a Valleys house - all sitting round - round tables etc. Children are allowed to be children and not constrained etc. It's pretty noisy at times..."

Other respondents identified the extended family patterns as a significant opportunity in rural areas:

"We have worked mainly through family lines as these are very close in a strong Welsh environment. The farming community and family lines make it a close-knit community."

Here, the relationships and the social life of the church were influential in the wider community. Once people joined the church community, they tended to stay, and their extended family were also drawn in. However, to reach such communities, it was essential to be a part of them. This was particularly the case in rural communities where family links through farming were stronger.

"But this can also be difficult in evangelising in the villages as people can be closed off to anybody new!"

In these situations, "proving yourself" was essential, and building stable and long-term relationships was the only way to gain a hearing.

It is in relation to the distinctive social patterns within Wales that Evangelistic churches have faced significant challenges. The effect of Pietism on the mission of E1 churches in particular, has, as Chambers observed, "done nothing to help their cause".[116] In communities where mutual help was part of the culture, a policy of separation, and a reliance on invitations to services and events within the church building, had isolated churches from the sphere of their mission. In some Valleys contexts, to be detached as a church was decidedly counter-cultural. The

---

116 Chambers, "Out of Taste," 92.

very rapid decline of Nonconformity in the post-industrial Valleys may be a consequence of this. One church that had changed from E1 to E2 expressed the dilemma:

> "The history of churches like (name), has tended to react against the social gospel and ended up throwing the baby out with the bathwater. So even now, in the last few years, we have really seen the importance of mercy ministries and social involvement in the church, as a valid thing for the church to do. It's not evangelism, but it is important to do."

The *Waleswide* Survey demonstrated that E2 churches, that are active in the community, are the ones seeing their church's mission lead to new members. In the Valleys, in line with the average across Wales, 46% of 5:2 churches had seven or more connections to their communities. *Foodbank*, *Christians Against Poverty* (CAP) debt projects, night shelters and community provision of nurseries, after-school clubs, parenting courses as well as support for families in crisis, were going with the grain of society and not against it. One church in the Merthyr Valley was involved in a night shelter for the homeless, CAP debt counselling, a drop-in centre, toddlers groups, *Foodbank*, and working with *Barnardo's* in adoption and fostering support. The church had grown from a core group of twenty people to a morning congregation of more than 120 between 2005 and 2014.

The traditional structures of E1 churches, where mission was centripetal not centrifugal, was not well geared for a mission of social care. Therefore, in traditional rural areas, and especially in Welsh language areas, churches that were evangelistic in intent were generally declining because of isolation from their communities. Of the 29 churches in rural areas, with an Evangelistic *Approach* to mission, only three were E2, of which two were growing 5:2.

Adjusting to the particular social patterns of Welsh contexts would seem to be not only essential for the future, but also a possible explanation of the decline of the recent past. This is especially the case for churches with patterns of mission from a Christendom era, which have not responded to changing religious and social patterns.

Adjusting to the Political Aspects of Welsh Context

The first decade of the twenty-first century was a time when Welsh institutions increased in number and influence. The National Assembly for Wales received additional powers, *Plaid Cymru* governed in a coalition, and Wales, as one of the Home Nations, became an accepted reality. In the questionnaire responses of churches with an Evangelistic *Approach* to mission, however, there was little awareness of, and few references to, the political aspects of context. Therefore, in the subsequent interviews, a specific question was included: "Are church members active in politics, and does the church encourage it?" This was explained in terms of a range from lobbying on political, moral or social issues, to involvement in local politics, to active participation in national politics (Chart 47). Of the twenty-nine leaders of Evangelistic churches, ten had no involvement at any level, thirteen were involved in lobbying, ten in local politics, and only four in national politics. Only two churches were involved at all levels. One church had a member standing as an independent local councillor, and only the two churches involved at all levels were actively encouraging people to be involved in politics. Such voices were unusual and exceptional.

> "Yes they are active in politics, (name) is a member who works for Care and has applied to become a County Councillor, and is applying to be an MEP. We are teaching our teenagers and young adults to engage in the political process. I am encouraging our twenty-somethings to become local councillors."

This comparatively low level of involvement in politics may have been, in part, a legacy of Pietist traditions, or it may have been a result of a low confidence that political action would produce the kind of change in society they were looking for. In the Valleys general disinterest in politics reflected a disappointment, or disillusion, with the Socialism that had been so dominant a generation earlier.

> "I don't think people have got any conviction that Socialism, or the Red, is ever going to achieve anything for us. Our champion was essentially the reason why the Tories and Margaret Thatcher got into power again. With Labour, if they had got anybody in at the helm apart from Neil, they may have had a chance, but our champion was unelectable in the eyes of the vast majority of the UK. He was this thick sounding Valley boy, too red, even his hair was red. As the last representative of Valleys socialism he achieved nothing."

Of those interviewed, some spoke of the legacy of Welsh history, "industrial abuse", English oppression, and an "underdog mentality", but were not politically active in response. Two English churches in mid Wales spoke of grievance against the Welsh Assembly Government and Welsh language education, but had made no political response either. Some Welsh speakers saw it as their duty to work for "their rights, their kids' education, university education and general recognition", but did so through direct action, not the political process.

Others had members with strong political views, but were not involved in politics as a church, nor encouraged support for one political party. Any alignment with nationalist politics, and activism in relation to issues of the Welsh language, may have more to do with the individuals and churches being Welsh-speaking than their Evangelistic *Approach* to mission. Certainly, in the interviews, there was no sense given that these activities were in any way an opportunity for Evangelistic endeavour.

Involvement in local or national politics, with few exceptions, involved praying for elected officials, or lobbying on Christian and ethical issues, where it was felt that a Christian viewpoint needed to be registered or defended. With such levels of political engagement, most of the churches with an Evangelistic *Approach* to mission did not see the political context of Wales as a sphere for active involvement, or something to adjust to significantly as an expression of their mission.

Reflections on the Evangelistic *Approach*

Churches and leaders with an Evangelistic *Approach* to mission had the proclamation of their message as their primary purpose for mission. Social action was, essentially, a consequence or a means to that end.

> "I understand the mission of the church is evangelism. That social works are not the mission of the church, but nonetheless we are as Christians called to love our neighbours as ourselves, and to serve others. That is what we are as Christians."

Adjustments to the six aspects of context in Wales, therefore, were necessary in order to make the proclamation effective. Evangelistic churches, especially E2, made changes in order to better communicate their message. They had a primary purpose for which traditions needed to be sacrificed if necessary. As a result the forms of evangelism, and the number and variety of connections to community, were greater than among churches for whom these activities were their sole focus. The community connections were an attempt, in the case of E2, to model the message, to give it credibility, and to provide a connection with the intended hearers. The lack of such a connection in E1 churches was seen to hinder their achieving the desired outcomes of their mission.

The Liberal *Approach* to Mission

The Liberal *Approach* to mission was a response to the changing intellectual and social climate in the decades leading up to, and following, the start of the twentieth century. It was inspired by the Enlightenment and emphasised reason as the way to find truth. Its Modernist thinking produced an optimism and hope in the progress of mankind. Its missiology was a social gospel, embracing many of the aspirations and principles of the emerging Socialism of the day.[117] It had an anti-supernaturalism that made salvation in this world its primary focus, minimising or denying expectations of personal salvation. Evangelism was regarded as a primitive and discriminatory activity belonging to the past. Tudur Jones outlines its assumptions:

> "To it, theology was a kind of philosophy, faith was a kind of reasoning, the Church was a kind of society, a miracle was a kind of natural uniformity, a prophet was a kind of genius, the Bible was a kind of literature, the Incarnation was a kind of evolution, the Atonement was a kind of martyrdom, and Jesus Christ's teaching was a fairly common set of principles".[118]

The leaders of the main denominations in Wales enthusiastically embraced the Liberal *Approach* to theology and mission.[119] Such views were all but obligatory for those in senior denominational positions, so that "theological liberalism had grown into being a kind of multifarious orthodoxy".[120] The teaching of the theological colleges shaped future ministry,[121] and the beliefs of the churches followed. Not all Nonconformists

---

117 Pope, *Building Jerusalem*, 5, 13-16; R. Pope, *Codi Muriau Dinas Duw: Anghydffurfiaeth ac Anghydffurfwyr Cymru'r Ugeinfed Ganrif* (Bangor: Prifysgol Cymru, 2005), 8.
118 Jones, *Congregationalism*, 239.
119 Pope, *Muriau*, 39-44; Jones, *Faith*, 194-197; Pope, *Building Jerusalem*, 14-15, 40-45.
120 Jones, *Congregationalism*, 240.
121 Pope, *Muriau*, 40; Jones, *Congregationalism*, 239.

in Wales adopted the new theology, but those who held to the former Evangelical traditions were few, especially among ministers.

However, the early confidence was shaken by the economic woes of the 1930s and its expectations were then seen as a forlorn hope, "dashed to pieces on the rocks of two world wars". Its beneficial results were sparse. Morgan, reviewing Welsh Nonconformity over the twentieth century, spoke of it "running into the sand", with "a disillusioned generation of ministers who, at the close of their ministry, have witnessed massive and disheartening decline".[122] This is particularly true in the Welsh language sections of the historic denominations, where the Liberal *Approach* had survived the longest. Welsh-speaking preachers were leaving a spiritual wilderness behind them. Hirsch called it a "parasitical ideology" because it "rarely creates new forms of church or extends Christianity in any significant way, but rather exists and 'feeds off' what the more orthodox missional movements started. Theological liberalism always comes later in the history of a movement, and it is normally associated with its decline."[123]

What the Questionnaire and Interviews showed

Charts 27 and 28 show that 39 churches could be identified as having a Liberal understanding of local church mission. Of these, 18% were in the 5:2 category, which was a lower proportion than all other *Approaches*. It is significant that none of the seven 5:2 Liberal churches had actually grown numerically. They had seen new people attending, but these additions had been outstripped by losses.

122 D. Morgan, *The Span of the Cross: Christian Religion and Society in Wales 1914–2000* (2nd; 1999; repr., Cardiff: University of Wales Press, 2011), xiv.
123 Hirsch, *Forgotten*, 262.

Churches, with a Liberal *Approach* to mission, saw social action as expressing the essential message and mission of the Church. As a result, responses to the questionnaire on how the local church's message was communicated included: "no direct outreach programmes", "no methods of evangelising as such", and "very little evangelistic or community outreach outside of children and youth work". The mission of the church was practical serving, not proclamation: "We see our primary mission as acting as channels of God's love to the world. It is not our purpose to bring people into Church on Sunday".

The absence of evangelism was, in part, due to the traditional nature of Liberal churches. The majority had retained the outward forms and ministry patterns of nineteenth century Welsh Nonconformity. This had a number of aspects. Firstly, any outreach generally was through an invitation to church services, sometimes via a church website. Mission was also seen in terms of changes to the services, such as through video presentation, or other contemporary media: "Our evangelism has changed little. We have modern hymn books, modern video and DVD Bible studies, but I would like to introduce Power Point in the services". These changes reflect a centripetal not centrifugal mission. Likewise, the high use of Services in the churches' connections to their communities, and especially how they "most" connected (Chart 48), shows a building centred approach. The responses also show fewer connections being "most used", suggesting that most connections were used occasionally, and not regularly (Chart 49).

The role of the paid minister was central to mission outside the church's walls, notably through visitation, weddings and funerals:

> "Yesterday is the mother of today in our evangelising. The burden falls on the minister's shoulders. Having the attitude that he is employed, and should earn his pay".

Where there was no minister, the mission of the church was seen as limited thereby:

> "The church has not had the benefit of a church minister and so has merely just ticked over and maintained regular Sunday worship, maintenance of buildings, token mission by way of a weekly Coffee shop and mutual support for the church members. There has been no evangelism because we had no expertise within the church to carry it out".

This ageing demographic of the churches also affected the ability of others to do mission: "Unfortunately, the people are elderly and just enjoy being together whether it be on a Sunday morning or a coffee morning/afternoon tea to raise money for charities". As a result, some saw very little community engagement.

The charts, which compare Liberal churches' connections to their communities with other *Approaches* (Charts 39 to 45), show the comparatively high use of church, youth and café related activities. This traditional mission pattern, centred on a church building, had a lower involvement in Need and Family activities. The lower use of Youth activities would reflect the ageing demographic. The cafés involved the church building being opened at specific times as a drop-in centre, largely as a meeting-point for the elderly, although one church did run a separate café in its village.

The greater use of Learning activities, than all other *Approaches* to mission, especially in the use of more than one activity, reflected the fact that more than half of the Liberal churches were Welsh-speaking, with cultural meetings and language classes as a part of church life, reflecting the close link between language and culture. This use of Learning Related connections was seen most clearly in the "most used" responses (Chart 46).

The Liberal Message and Means of Communication

The Liberal *Approach* to mission was more concerned with social and political issues than a proclaimed message. The message that was declared was a general one, about the love of God to all people, being non-discriminatory in its welcome to all:

- "[We are] an inclusive Christian fellowship. In being inclusive it does not discriminate against those it welcomes and serves, showing concern, friendship and love".

- "The greatest commandment ... love God and love your neighbour, everything hangs on this. That is our primary statement which informs the rest of what we do in the church.

- "I would call myself a progressive Christian, and I try to include that in my messages... that we are all children of God, we are all absolutely equal... and we are just part of the planet, not in charge of it. I try to plug all these things: Green, environmental, respect for all life".

- "That God so loved the world, and that means the world, all the people in the world. Christ came to give his life, knowledge, and fullness in this world as well. ... 'The common good', and that's it to me".

- "We are open to proclaim the good news of Jesus Christ, and hope. But everyone is accepted and loved by God".

- "That we are a welcoming and inclusive kingdom community. Radical welcome and inclusive and the community of people committed to the values of love and mercy, inclusion and diversity, and all of that. We do have a mission strapline, 'Open to the world, supporting each other, centred on God'.

This general message, of God's benevolence to all in the world, does not call individuals to a personal salvation. This is clearly a significant factor in the lack of additions to Liberal churches, and of their relentless decline.

This message was largely communicated in and through church activities in a church building. This was reflected in the use of the various approaches to communicating their message (Chart 50): preaching, Sunday School and ministerial visitation. The relatively low use of a second approach within each category (Chart 51) underlines that the single use was often the work of the paid minister. The very low use of "Relational" approaches shows the reliance on church services, with less use of activities outside the church building. The responses, showing how people came to faith (Chart 52), also reflected the influence of the work of the minister, and the emphasis on activities in the church building. Growth, where it did occur, was largely by the addition of family members, or resulted from parents following their children to church. Unlike other *Approaches*, the use of evangelistic missions, guest services, meals and courses was low. In fact, responses were lower in all categories except one, when compared to the other *Approaches* to mission (Chart 38). Liberal churches saw fewer additions.

The influence of pastoral visiting by the minister was the exception in this picture. Liberal churches used this Direct method to communicate their message more than other *Approaches* (Chart 35 and 36), and outsiders became church attenders through it (Chart 52). Liberal churches did not see canvassing for new members as part of their mission. Therefore, home visitation would not involve door-to-door evangelistic visitation by members or the minister. The traditional role of the minister in pastoral visitation of the sick, the house bound, and after births or funerals attracted people to church, especially in rural areas. The great majority of

Liberal churches were in rural or small town situations where community relations remained strong, and where the chapel, and its minister, still had a perceived relevance.

Despite this sphere of success, however, the mission activities of Liberal churches were limited in their effectiveness. There was an awareness that the absence of outward-looking mission was threatening the very future of the churches.

> "There will be changes, but as far as the Welsh churches are concerned, if it isn't a change in the way that we reach out, our responsibility is to reach out, then we are going to grow weaker and weaker".

For others the extent of decline had gone too far to be remedied. They were aware of other growing churches, but were either unwilling, or unable, to follow their example. The need for change was expressed by other leaders, and some saw a possible future if mission to the community could be embraced:

> "I don't know if there is another generation ...that will sit down, come to the meeting, and listen to the sermon, and be very faithful. ... To stay in the tradition is easy, but to break free of the tradition is a step into the unknown.... We must initiate and take risk. As ministers we won't succeed when we don't take risks".

However, conservatism and traditionalism were shaping the mission of most Liberal churches. It was reflected in their growth patterns, as well as their engagement in mission. An emphasis on engaging with social trends from the pulpit had affected attitudes to politics and theology, but in most cases had not led to a practical mission addressing needs outside the chapel walls. The Liberal expression of mission was coming to an end as the research was being conducted. Ministers were leaving their ministry or reaching retirement age, with little prospect of a successor in most cases, as ageing congregations declined towards closure.

Adjusting the Religious Aspects of Welsh Context

The Liberal *Approach* to mission, with its social gospel, was an innovative and *avant garde* response to the post-war situation in Wales, early in the twentieth century. Socialism was in its ascendancy, industrial decline was threatening, and communities were in economic crisis. It sought to bring a good news that was practical, and more relevant to current needs, than the Church's traditional message. Chapels were valued as an accepted part of Welsh national life, but when the new message failed to produce either a renewal of the chapels, or an effective answer to the social problems being addressed, decline was unabated.

A number of factors, relating to the religious context of Wales, give some explanation for the disappointing outcomes. Firstly, Liberal churches assumed that there would be an ongoing connection, and loyalty, between the local communities and the chapel. Affection may have remained, but loyalty did not:

> "I've spoken to a few who don't have any connection with the church and they would find its closure unacceptable. It is part of their psyche, and is important to them, whether they realise it or not. It is part of their Welshness".

People might view the religious legacy positively, but for many it was merely a "hand-me-down" that permeated families, leaving a sense of association that was otherwise "quite irrelevant to the people outside at the moment". Society around the churches had changed, and although there was a lingering memory of chapel loyalty, there was no meaningful connection: "you still have a lot of people who know which Chapel they don't go to".

Secondly, this conservatism produced an aversion to change, when the society around the chapel was changing exponentially:

> "...a little reluctant to accept change or do change ... I think that some of the churches, probably this one included, I don't see how it will still be here quite honestly, because we have an older congregation. ... I just can't see it continuing".

Both the preservation of typical Welsh chapel forms, as well as a reluctance to modernise, were seen as typically Welsh. Their influence in society was mainly one of nostalgia. This was particularly evident in Welsh language churches where "yesterday is the mother of today in our evangelising". The core problem was described as the Chapel culture, with "more respect for the building than for Christ", in a world where "Sunday is for sport, not God". Society had changed around them, with the result that the chapels were left in a backwater, largely unconnected to contemporary society.

> "They have not moved on you know. In Chapel, in church life, there is something very old-fashioned. ... if someone who died 100 years ago came back today the only place you'll (recognise) is the Welsh Chapel".

As a result, younger generations were seen to have "given up on the influence. It is part of their grandfather's generation, not theirs", so that youth and the employed generations had largely broken free from chapel obligations.

Thirdly, the resulting isolation of the chapels meant that there was an inability to communicate the church's message. The Liberal message, of how God's love could change the human condition, was heard only within chapel walls.[124] When asked how people would hear this message, leaders were aware of a fundamental dis-connect. The only way people would hear the message was:

"By coming. They wouldn't otherwise. It sounds very negative, the only way they would hear our message is through seeing what we try to do with community work... Christian Aid collection outside Tesco every year. That doesn't seem very innovative does it?"

Fourthly, despite the radical change to a social agenda in the churches' message, mission remained building centred, and centripetal not centrifugal. Without changes that would take mission into the community, the prospects were bleak. One leader, with two chapels on the point of closure, hoped the buildings would become a community garden, and the church re-form under lay leadership. The Liberal *Approach* to mission had not only failed to transform the wider society, but its inability to attract new, younger, members was leading to its own demise.

"They (the members) have lost a lot in terms of the decline of the church... There will be no church. There will be no church".

As a commentary on a particular approach to church, theology, and mission, these comments are stark and announce the end of an era. Liberal churches had wedded their mission to a Christendom model of mission, where people needed to come, rather than the church needed to go. The Liberal churches had neither a mission nor a message that would inspire people to want to be part of their church. Moving away from Welsh Nonconformity's theological heritage, and its proclamation in evangelism, meant that the disappearing generation was not being replaced in the churches.

---

124 "I can't say that there are many that have been brought into Christianity, but a lot of people have been brought to think about the concept of love that Jesus talked about. Perhaps that's enough because when they asked Jesus he didn't say anything about himself, just to love God and love your neighbour. So perhaps that is enough, I don't know".

Adjusting to the Geographic Aspects of Welsh Context

Leaders of churches with a Liberal *Approach* to mission were aware of the importance of identity being linked to locality. Loyalty to village or valley was again seen as stronger than to a national identity.

> "In the area there is a greater loyalty to locality than to the national. ... we tend to be more parochial, *plwyfol*, more concerned with our *milltir sgwar* (square mile)...They only think about their patch".

The tradition of Nonconformist chapel, that the Liberal *Approach* to mission relied on, had been ubiquitous in Wales. As a result, the local chapel served a particular denominational constituency within a defined local area. Its boundaries were set by the next chapel, which served an adjacent community. As a result, chapels had their own version of localism, reflecting that fashioned by landforms and social features. By the end of the twentieth century, this localism had been weakened by declining membership, but ageing members would still retain their membership, and return to the family chapel for worship, if such a journey was physically possible. For such commuting members, living in one place but worshiping in another, mission to the chapel's hinterland was difficult, if not impossible.

Rural patterns were less evident in or near urban areas. However, one Welsh church near Cardiff deliberately met a demand for a rural atmosphere among Welsh speakers, who travelled out from the city. Another provided a church community in the city, treating Welsh speakers as a village community within the city:

> "In one way you could look upon the Welsh chapels in a place like (place) as people in a village... They come to meet one another on weeknights, and afternoons, and on Sundays to worship, and that is their social context for many of them... in one sense that is their village".

Another influence of localism was a felt need to maintain a chapel within its community. Because of the strong identity with a local community or location, the amalgamation of chapels in a central location did not satisfy local desires. One church with a Liberal *Approach* to mission actually reopened a chapel in order to satisfy the needs of that community. Such a policy would seem appropriate to context, assuming people and resources permitted it, as opposed to the building of large churches and centres designed to serve large rural areas.

Adjusting to the Ethnic Aspects of Welsh Context

Liberal Churches, in maintaining a traditional Nonconformist expression of church and mission, related most naturally to rural or Welsh language communities. The approach was less suitable in areas that had seen significant inward migration from England, and its traditional approach heightened awareness of the difference between traditional Welsh and contemporary English societies. To Liberal leaders, especially those from Welsh language churches, the two communities represented distinct and separate *ethnies*. A Welsh-speaking minister described the difference, and their apparent separation from each other:

> "If you ask people in the street are you Welsh, yes! But I don't know what is meant by it. They would not watch S4C. It would be the Anglo-American culture, they are in Wales, brought up in a Welsh community, I don't know these people, and I don't mix with them, our worlds don't meet".

The perceived differences between these two groups had certain implications for mission according to Liberal leaders. Liberal mission, especially in rural areas, focussed predominantly on the Welsh *ethnie*, whilst evidently resenting the new residents in the area. They spoke of

117

differences of psyche as well as linguistic and cultural differences. The Welsh were seen as more reticent, afraid to take the lead in case they offended someone else, "Nobody wants to take the lead, and no one wants to be seen as *Ceffyl Blaen* (the leading horse), as it were. ... Are they more subservient? Stuck in a rut?" A feeling of being the "underdog", even in their own church, resulted. The English in-comers were seen as more confident and assertive, even "cheeky", and as taking over in the community.

> "We try to connect to those of the original community and the incomers. It is the in-comer, the person who is ready to move on, who is the activist. Some feel that they are taking over...".

In English-speaking areas, the influx of English members into churches was producing internal tension. The new-comers from England were not only assuming the leadership of the church and mission, but also deterring the original members from doing so. As a result, the "Welsh see the English as like a bull-at-a-gate, the others say, 'These Welsh never get on with it'" This leader spoke of resentment as the chapel community was being spoilt, and that the family chapel was being taken over. Churches and their mission, that had become English in leadership and style, would be seen as alien by the local community, and thus isolated from it. One leader wished that the Welsh would show more "backbone", and bemoaned a lack of self-belief.

The change was exacerbated by the depopulation of traditional Welsh areas, and the inward migration of those retiring to country and coastal areas. As the Liberal churches were predominantly within the Welsh communities, which were diminishing in number and influence, the implications for mission were considerable. One leader described the situation and challenge graphically:

"Unfortunately there are two communities, there are so many incomers now that form their own community which doesn't have much to do with the local Welsh. As you find, especially in local Wales, the English are more aggressive in their attitudes and more confident and take over the institutions, the village hall for example has been taken over..."

This Liberal leader implied a fortress mentality, where the Welsh community was threatened by the incomers. The church, and its mission, were also being demoralised and lacking in initiative. A lack of desire and ability to serve the wider community in mission followed inevitably.

The churches with a Liberal *Approach* to mission, therefore, had only related to one *ethnie* in an era when Wales was experiencing rapid inward migration, and where few areas could be described as mono-ethnic. At the same time, the Welsh *ethnie* itself was morphing under the influence of secularism, electronic media, and multi-nationalism, so that the Liberal *Approach* to mission, even in its target group, was increasingly ineffective.

Adjusting to the Linguistic and Cultural Aspects of Welsh Context

The close connection between Liberal churches and traditional Welsh identity was expressed in a shared Welsh language and culture. Although the Liberal social gospel was initially concerned with political and social need issues, it was as a defender of the Welsh language, and its associated culture, especially in the face of its decline, that their mission was focussed at the beginning of the twenty-first century.

"It's always been a struggle, and it's much more of a struggle in recent years. They are in a state of panic really when they realise this reality of the situation. They don't like it at all".

Mission to Welsh language communities involved the provision of Welsh-only worship, advocacy of simultaneous translation in meetings, support for Welsh schools and Welsh learning, the promotion of *eisteddfodau*, choirs, a drama society, Welsh services in care homes, and the promotion of Welsh culture and history through classes and discussion groups. These activities support and defend Welsh language and culture, as "all serve to plant seeds in lives that can then grow". The comparatively high use of the Learning group of community connections by Liberal churches, described earlier, is reflected in some of these activities.

A Welsh church, in a pre-dominantly English-speaking area, had deliberately changed from bilingual services to Welsh-only, rather than to English-only, in order to reach the local Welsh community. To do so had been "a bit of a challenge ... and to keep at it took real effort at times", because such a step was contrary to community trends. However, with the rise in Welsh-medium education, and Welsh people moving into the area, the step was taken out of a sense of responsibility for the language and culture:

> "This is important to the church, because it is very conscious of its responsibility to secure the Welsh language heritage as well as the Welsh heritage in the town ... What has developed is that the community the church serves is the church community. It is not being insular in that sense but is seeing itself as serving this community that wants to live its life through the medium of Welsh... The language, the culture, everything involved with that culture, the Chapel being at the hub of it".

In such communities, whether in Welsh or English language areas, the language was the key to mission. Such an approach, however, deliberately excluded the participation of English speakers, and mission to them: "the vast majority of members would not countenance English in the life of the church. Therefore if somebody is not Welsh-speaking it would be difficult for them to fit".

The mission by Liberal churches, through promoting and defending Welsh language and culture, was for the perceived benefit of society, rather than an attempt to increase congregations. In one city church, this had clearly been an unexpected consequence, as the chapel became a focal point of the wider Welsh-speaking community. Elsewhere, however, the churches were tending to decline with the language and traditional culture. At the start of the twenty-first century the defence and promotion of the language was increasingly in secular hands, and the chapels marginalised. As a result, churches with a Liberal *Approach* to mission, active in the spheres of language and culture, were declining more rapidly than the causes they were seeking to defend.

Adjusting to the Social Aspects of Welsh Context

In Welsh language churches, there was a strong sense of Welsh language community, as those communities used the chapel as a focal point for social and family activity. This was seen as particularly important in urban areas, where it was adding to the churches' influence.

> "In (town) the Welsh language chapels are still important to the Welsh Community. They are still influential, with community life in them ... Their influence is greater in the city".

There were, however, some Welsh language rural communities where interaction between chapel and community would still be a daily experience, where family and work relationships were interwoven, like "one big family", with an extensive awareness of people and their family connections over generations.

This connection with community was weaker in English language areas, except for the drop-in centres and cafés provided for the community, especially the elderly. These centres were open to all, "an accepting, relaxed non-judgmental environment which reflects the attitude of Christ". Liberal churches were at pains not to discriminate, though it was acknowledged that the inclusiveness had led to "an issue of nominalism" arising from "a cultural understanding of chapel life".

These community connections centred on the use of their buildings, often by local organisations using them. Connections in the community would be through the work of the minister, doing funerals, home and hospital visitation, and running activities for children. Some churches contributed to a local *Foodbank*, or similar ecumenical initiative, but few were actively involved in other need-orientated mission. This was seen most clearly in the "most used" connections to their communities (Chart 49), which showed what approaches would be used regularly, rather than occasionally. The age profile of Liberal churches would now make activity in the community a challenge, and is a factor in the recorded decline of Liberal churches.

Adjusting to the Political Aspects of Welsh Context

In the nineteenth century Welsh Nonconformity had given the *gwerin* of Wales a democratic voice within the chapel community, and a collective voice to Government, when no Welsh political structures existed. The Liberal churches developed and defended this tradition, and their social gospel had a political agenda. Churches encouraged their members to be active in political process at local and national level:

"The church had been important in a civic sense, with mayors in the church. They were very powerful people. You had this element among the *Annibynwyr* to be involved in politics, more than with any other denomination".

Liberal churches spoke of activism among their members, and of the presence of elected officials in the congregation, including the family of the First Minister of the National Assembly of Wales. MPs, AMs, and local councillors were members of the churches, although some respondents said that that there were fewer than in previous years.

Leaders said that they did not advocate a particular party from the pulpit, and that their church encouraged political action, not party politics, however, some churches said that their members were known for their political flavour. Political activism among members was strongest in Welsh language churches, where support for *Plaid Cymru* predominated. An awareness of Wales' loss of freedom, prosperity and representation under English rule was expressed repeatedly.

"The castle reminds us of oppression, but we've got it now! It led to an uncertainty, lack of self-belief. Always kept down, slow to take responsibility ... It reminds you of yesterday, and that is still there".

However, the presence of the National Assembly of Wales was said to be giving new confidence.

Churches in the south Wales Valleys, however, expressed their support for the Labour Party, which was rooted in a similar sense of grievance for perceived exploitation by England, this time in the industrial sphere.

"There is a feeling that we have been robbed by the English. This is true in the industrial Valleys, where they came in and took the profit ... The amount of hatred that there still is, and it is hatred for Maggie... because she closed the mines. She is not liked. At the cinema when Churchill came on they used to boo him, because he sent the troops into Tonypandy. They've got long memories..."

However, political support for Labour in the Valleys was not as strong as in previous generations. One leader spoke of a huge sense of disillusion, especially in younger generations, stemming from the mine closures and the failure of trade unions to stop it.

Despite these reservations, the Liberal *Approach* to mission emphasised political involvement, and encouraged involvement at all levels of politics. They had the highest level of involvement at national level of all the *Approaches* to mission, reflecting their involvement and engagement with the governments in Westminster and Cardiff (Chart 47).

Political action at a local level involved representation and lobbying by members, together with supporting "Christian Aid, *Foodbank*, work for refugees...", "Campaigning on social issues, poverty, equality", "towards the world, to justice and to world peace, and that is part of our mission". In Welsh language churches it also involved support for *Cymdeithas yr Iaith*, and in direct action against holiday cottages in Welsh areas, painting them with black paint. Ironically, the cottages were owned by fellow members of the same chapel. The event divided church members as well as the village.

If political activism was declining in Liberal churches, it was because Liberal churches were ageing, declining and closing. The benefits of their political activity for those outside the churches might have been great and lasting, but it did not sustain the numerical strength of the churches, whose decline meant that the mission, and its benefits, faded.

Reflections on the Liberal *Approach*

The Liberal *Approach* to mission, being closely aligned to traditional Welsh culture, often in its rural form, was sometimes successful, but within a narrowing sphere. Its social and political message, and its defence of Welshness, reflected the aspirations and priorities of its ageing ministers and members. The desire to serve local geographical and linguistic communities, and to provide pastoral care to them through well trained ministers, was not sufficient to ensure an ongoing influence, legacy or future. The loyalty to tradition might not have been open to negotiation: "I am a traditional missioner ... God is a Welshman!", and such sentiments might be applauded within the chapel, but they were increasingly meaningless in the wider community. This *Approach* to mission relied on the religious context of a Christianised Wales, where people came to chapel without being sought. A failure to adjust to the changing religious context in Wales meant that their mission would, inevitably, be short-lived, for them and for those that they sought to serve. The Liberal *Approach* to mission was "out of taste and out of time".[125]

---

125 Chambers, "Out of Taste," 86.

The *Missio Dei Approach* to Mission

The *Missio Dei Approach* to mission is normally associated with the name of Lesslie Newbigin. He was born in 1909, educated in a Quaker school, ordained as a missionary of the Church of Scotland, and became a bishop in the ecumenical "Church of South India".[126] His was an eclectic, ecumenical approach to mission. Though he had an Evangelical leaning, he also questioned the authority of the Bible and saw doctrine and truth as fluid, and needing contextual revision.[127] He spoke of the tensions between Liberals and Evangelicals as a "deep and tragic split" and a "destructive conflict", and so looked for an ecumenical middle way.

On his retirement in 1974 he returned to the UK, where his career took a remarkable turn. In 1983, he wrote a small book, *The Other Side of 1984*,[128] which became an unexpected best seller. It led to the founding of the "Gospel and Our Culture" network. Newbigin contended for a three-fold Trinitarian mission, the *Missio Dei Approach*.[129] God was at work in his world, so mission had to engage in the secular spheres of justice, poverty and environment, in Jesus' name. Evangelism was to be at the centre of mission,[130] but social involvement, with ethical overtones, was the main element.[131] God's salvation involves political, cultural and spiritual engagement with His world. Mission is no longer simply to flow out of an emphasis on Jesus' Great Commission (Matthew 28:19-20), but from an

---

126 P. Weston, ed., *Lesslie Newbigin, Missionary Theologian: a Reader* (Grand Rapids: Eerdmans, 2006), 5-7.
127 J. E. L. Newbigin, *The Open Secret* (Grand Rapids: Eerdmans, 1983), 173-180; Weston, *Newbigin*, 213-215.
128 Weston, *Newbigin*, 189-197.
129 Newbigin, *Secret*, 20-31; J. E. L. Newbigin, *The Gospel in a Pluralist Society* (London: SPCK, 1989), 118-120; Weston, *Newbigin*, 81-3; Keller, *Center*, 251-252.
130 Newbigin, *Secret*, 136, 146.
131 Newbigin, *Secret*, 102, 103, 152.

awareness that the three persons of the Trinity were integrally involved in mission in all of God's world. Newbigin distinguished between the proclamation of the gospel and the wider mission.

The local church was to be "the hermeneutic of the gospel" as it lived out all aspects of God's mission, as "God's embassy", representing God in his world.[132] He believed that the Church needed to rethink completely its strategy in a post-Christendom context. It now had a peripheral voice, and was to regain influence by challenging the credibility of secularism, and "reclaim the high ground of public truth".[133] Europe was not a society which had no gods, but a society which had false gods. This society was far more resistant to the gospel than a society with no previous Christian history, and was "the most challenging missionary frontier of our time".[134]

Newbigin's thinking was developed by David Bosch[135] who saw mission in a similar Trinitarian framework, giving it wider redemptive scope in the world as a comprehensive salvation.[136] The Church was to participate in what God was doing in society today rather than focus on individual salvation.[137] Mission, as the extending rule of God, was viewed as being greater than the Church. Where Bosch went further than Newbigin was to suggest that mission, as an expression of God's wider work in the world, and that evangelism was to consist of "alerting people to the reign of God" not "recruitment to religion".[138]

In local church mission, this Trinitarian mission would involve the churches in "Community Transformation" in which they were to

---

132 Newbigin, *Pluralist*, 184.
133 Newbigin, *Pluralist*, 232-233.
134 J. E. L. Newbigin, *Foolishness to the Greeks* (London: SPCK, 1986), 20.
135 Notably in his *Transforming Mission* (Maryknoll: Orbis, 2009).
136 Bosch, *Transforming*, 390, 399-408, 493,
137 Bosch, *Transforming*, 84, 90, 98, 253.
138 D. J. Bosch, *Believing in the Future* (Leominster: Gracewing, 1995), 33, 58.

be involved in all community programmes.[139] Duncan, in explaining community transformation, equated the kingdom of God with social action, meaning a "felt change in our communities and our world",[140] especially in contending for justice and righteousness.[141] In emphasising the social nature of the kingdom of God, evangelism is not prioritised, "notching up converts" is derogated, and repentance and conversion are regarded in social terms.[142]

What the Questionnaire and Interviews showed

In Wales, *Missio Dei* churches spoke of their ecumenical connections for mission and of partnerships with other churches in a "cross-church activity". The *Missio Dei Approach* was on the wide scope of its mission, rather than a narrow message. Charts 27 and 28 show that forty five churches could be identified as having a *Missio Dei* understanding of local church mission. Of these, 27% were in the 5:2 category. The 45 churches consisted of 36 churches from the historic denominations, and nine newer churches. The traditional churches had accepted the ecumenical *Missio Dei* commitments of their denominations, or at least their leaders had, which meant an acceptance, in principle, of the need for such mission. However, active involvement in the mission was not always evident.

> "Most people in my church would not see the need to engage with the community. They expect people to come to church (not for us go to the people) ... The chapel matters more than the kingdom".

139 McClymond, "Mission and Evangelism," in McDermott, *Evangelical Theology*, 7; M. Duncan, *Kingdom Come: The Local Church as a Catalyst for Social Change* (Oxford: Monarch, 2007), 322-323.
140 Duncan, *Kingdom Come*, 21.
141 Duncan, *Kingdom Come*, 18-19, 179, 189, 195.
142 Duncan, *Kingdom Come*, 21, 30, 72, 76-77, 200, 212, 324.

Others spoke of an initial reluctance to be involved in such a change, followed by limited progress to becoming outward looking.

It was, largely, the newer churches, together with some Charismatic Baptist churches that had moved away from traditional patterns, which had got involved practically in such mission to their communities. These were churches which, separating mission and evangelism, were prioritising social action. They sought to provide services without any underlying evangelistic connection. One church commented on its absence:

> "Whereas the church is very active in "outreach" ministries - both regular activities with the young and caring ministries such as *foodbank* and CAP - actual 'evangelistic endeavours' seem to be lacking".

Another church saw their change in mission approach to be a deliberate turning away from evangelistic programmes and activity.

Missio Dei churches engaged with their communities simply for the good of the community. They made consistent reference to their community involvement for its own sake, without reference to evangelism. They expressed a desire to meet the needs of their community over the long-term, so that the church became "just very much part of the community". The churches had researched the needs of their communities and responded to meet the identified needs. They provided services such as a community coffee shop, pre-school nursery, meeting point for the elderly, adult education classes, *Foodbank*, *Street* and *School Pastors*, feeding the roofless, support for families with addiction problems, and furniture recycling. One church chose to be involved in a pregnancy advice service, because their town was said to have the highest rate of teenage pregnancy in Europe, and in *Street Pastors* because the town was "key in the night economy". These activities, consistent with a *Missio Dei Approach*, were seen as representing kingdom activity, in contrast to activities that were evangelistic or church centred:

> "We are trying to learn and engage in being a kingdom influence / witness in our day-to-day lives. It's a struggle to change from activity / programme based evangelism but we believe it to be a vital element".

The motivation for such mission was not the enlargement of the local church, or the spiritual needs of the individual, but a desire to express and reflect God's mission of unconditional love for their community:

> "We do *foodbank* and communicate the love of God ... (it) carries the message to show how much God loves them ... by us being out there. In *foodbank* and furniture we are very upfront about why we do what we do, because of God's love ... We don't do these things to get people into church, that's not why we do it".

Missio Dei churches providing such services, had "good relationships with the police, town Council and job centre, social services" and schools. Two churches arranged all the local community activities, because of a lack of facilities or initiative from elsewhere. One of them also funded the initiatives:

> "We donate significant monies to community activities, e.g. Infant/Junior School in the Village, Playgroup, Village Hall. We support our local [Place] Festival Week and Carnival. We have run 'Party in the Park', an after-school celebration on our Football pitch, and focussed on local children, all funded totally by the Church ... and we believe we are respected for that".

These initiatives were done for purely altruistic reasons, and not intended for the direct, or indirect, benefit of the church. Another church focussed on care for the elderly, particularly through luncheon clubs, because of the age demographic of the area. They were also leading a night-shelter project outside their area, again without any specific evangelistic expectation: "We wait to see what comes out of it … We need to be light. … it has not been intentional, but rather waiting to see what comes out of it."

The traditional *Missio Dei* churches reflected an ecclesiology that was centred on a building and served by a minister as leader. This chapel tradition had shaped the mission approaches of the 36 denominational churches. It was reflected in the extent to which Church Related connections to community were utilised by *Missio Dei* churches (Chart 53). This reflected the fact that a *Missio Dei Approach*, in theory, may not always effect actual practice. This traditional pattern was also seen in the high use of youth, family and café activities for connection to community, where such connections would often be based in church buildings (Chart 53). When the "most used" connections were compared (Chart 54), it was evident that only church related activities had significant emphasis.

The charts, which compare *Missio Dei* churches' connections to their communities with other *Approaches* (Charts 39 to 45), show the comparatively high use of church, youth and café related activities. This traditional mission pattern of a majority of *Missio Dei* churches, centred on a church building, had been broadened by the activities of the newer churches and Charismatic Baptist churches. Without their broader involvement, *Missio Dei* church engagement in Need and Family activities would have been minimal.

The *Missio Dei* Message and Means of Communication

The *Missio Dei Approach*, like the Liberal *Approach*, stressed God's love and work in all of his world, but included personal salvation as one aspect. Their descriptions of their primary message reflected this:

- "The message is the kingdom in the community, to explain that Jesus is here, and about getting the community in we bring the kingdom wherever we go. Holiness is living Christ. The gospel is more than being converted and going to heaven, it's about justice and care".

- "I think the primary message now is that it is inclusive here as a family... We are seen as very much part of the community... The core message: The obvious message is the gospel, that Christ has come to give life and life in all its fullness, and that you won't find life in anything else".

- "Internally, the kingdom of God is at hand so repent and believe. We want to espouse a message that is kingdom orientated. Outside we espouse a message of social action, political action ... to talk about the good news of the church as a community, seeking to model a better way of living".

- "How much God loves them, and the opportunity to come to him. There is a response on our part too, of love".

- "That people are on a spiritual journey whether they believe it or not. They want to find meaning in life. We won't find that meaning until we actually find our Creator, and we won't find the creator unless we engage with those who are finding him, and his way of finding him is Jesus, and his love."

The underlying evangelistic roots of the non-traditional leaders is evident, but that message has been merged with a social action, or kingdom, agenda. This has led to a deliberate down playing of personal or individual salvation, seeing it as merely part of God's wider agenda. Such a lack of emphasis meant that additions were not being sought as a priority, and so were not evident.

The influence of the traditional chapel culture was reflected in how *Missio Dei* churches communicated their message (Charts 56 & 57). The charts show a use of Relational and Direct approaches to evangelism. However, traditional denominational churches, with a paid minister, relied heavily on this person for contact with the community, including home and hospital visitation. This would explain why these churches had a higher use of Relational and Direct approaches in general terms (Chart 55), but less so in "most used" (Chart 56). Church members did not tend to add to the minister's pastoral or evangelistic contacts with the community. One-man, or one-woman, ministry was still the dominant pattern in denominational churches, and particularly so in Welsh-speaking areas.

The pattern is seen most clearly in the means whereby people had come to faith, and had been added to the church (Chart 57), the church based activities of preaching, clubs and youth activities, together with the minister's role in conversation and visiting were dominant. When the use of church services was analysed for *Missio Dei* churches (Chart 58), there was a clear correlation between a reliance on Services to communicate the message, in one or more way, and whether a church was declining or growing. Such a reliance was a distinctive of declining *Missio Dei* churches.

Those relying on traditional church services and ministry in English-speaking communities, despite agreeing with a *Missio Dei Approach* to mission in principle, were not active in practice, and were declining. Those with an Evangelical or Charismatic tradition, whilst seeing their mission through social action as distinct from their evangelism, were mostly active, influential and, in some cases, growing.

Adjusting to the Religious Aspects of Welsh Context

The leaders of *Missio Dei* churches did not describe the Welsh religious context differently from other *Approaches*, but they did see it from different perspectives. Leaders from newer churches were not confined by traditional patterns, but those from a traditional denominational background had expressed the frustrations described earlier. The problem was also a direct result of an ageing demographic in the churches, which had led to them becoming detached from their communities, having "lost their right to be in a position of leadership in their community... They probably became too old to do anything about it by then".

The frustration and hopelessness expressed showed that there was little confidence in the inherited forms. A change in ecclesiology, and mission approach, was seen as an important part of the answer:

> "Welsh people have a negative impression of Church and overcoming these negative stereotypes, of who we are, is our greatest challenge".

The changes required for effective mission, which the less traditional churches had begun to implement, were seen as structural and theological. The structural changes involved a wholesale abandonment of traditional models of mission in favour of something relevant, contemporary and engaging. This involved changes in the mission as well as forms of services: "... by consistently demonstrating the love of Christ in action, and to have services which are actually more appealing than an hour of unnecessary dental surgery".

The theological changes involved a rejection of the convictions and practices of certain E1 churches. Leaders described the hindrance to mission in their area, as they saw it.

> "It is thick with Calvinism, which is a kind of spiritual insurance policy that

does not bless the Church... The chapels are dying on their feet because that Calvinism doesn't work in a world of mass media ... It's a club mentality, and it comes out of Calvinism, and a particular kind of Calvinism... the kind of fatalism".

These churches were engaging with their communities despite resistance, or a refusal to cooperate, from other churches. Their pragmatic and activist approach to mission emphasised human initiative and responsibility. They were seeking to cooperate, at a human level, with God's mission in their community.

Adjusting to the Geographic Aspects of Welsh Context

Missio Dei churches were situated in all regions of Wales, in rural and urban contexts, and in both language communities. They had the same understanding of Welsh localism, and, as a result, the churches' mission was limited to its immediate constituency. Churches identified with a local pride of place and targeted their community work within that defined sphere, rather than trying to enlarge it. A church on the edge of an estate with its own identity, that had changed from being council owned to private ownership, engaged exclusively with that community:

"... there is a strong connection with their very local community, who they feel called to serve and evangelise to. They do not cast their nets wide. ... It is to this context that the church feels called to serve, which is in the majority a white, English-speaking environment".

Another church saw its community as "a very large village, so everybody knows everybody", and suggested that the "small town feel" might be the essential feature of the area's Welshness. As a result, its extensive activities were focussed on this one community.

The *Missio Dei Approach* to mission was to serve communities for their own good, at the point of their need. Therefore, it was perhaps inevitable that this *Approach* emphasised its engagement with a specific local area. Needs in a wider area, or adjacent community, would be different, so *Missio Dei* churches tended to engage exclusively with their own immediate context.

Adjusting to the Ethnic Aspects of Welsh Context

Missio Dei churches sought to do mission to serve their whole community. As a result, when asked about the Welshness of people, they were quick to comment on the diversity of their surrounding population. A church in a border town spoke of the "split between English and Welsh who live here", and a leader in Pembrokeshire spoke of "Little England beyond Wales", commenting that,

> "... it most certainly isn't! It's quite a 'mongrel' community with a long military / dockyard history that means it is not traditionally Welsh [until it comes to rugby], but very distinctive in its own right, having more to do with southern Ireland, Cornwall and Brittany, than Cardiff, Treorchy or Aberystwyth".

A leader in Cardiff spoke of the community's cosmopolitan make-up, with people from many parts of Wales, but also other parts of the world. Others spoke of a variety of nationalities in their churches and communities, of "nine or ten nations represented on a Sunday", of groups from Nigeria, and in Wrexham of more Polish than Welsh speakers.

So strong was the awareness of bi-ethnicity, or multi-ethnicity, that exclusive attitudes to Welshness prompted concerns about racism.

"(Town) is a very mixed community - 7,000 residents and a lot of English immigration along with the indigenous community... We don't believe in "distinctly Welsh" or "distinctly English", such ideas lead easily to tribalism and racism. We are all mongrels".

Missio Dei leaders were very aware of the ethnic diversity of their communities, and some commented on the adverse effect that this had had on the local population. Some put the Welsh *ethnie* in sharper focus, speaking of a sense of inferiority, dourness, reserve and pessimism, "as if everyone else is better than they themselves. Either this or they blame the English for all their troubles". The original Welsh communities were seen to have a reserved trait which was the direct result of relatively recent inward migration of other ethnicities, especially for Welsh-speaking churches in predominantly English-speaking areas. One Welsh church leader spoke of "native Welsh" that had become a minority, and of "immigrants from the rest of Wales". Consequently, Welsh language *Missio Dei* churches conducted their mission to the Welsh-speaking population only, in a way that was particular to its language and minority mind-set: "We are aware of who we are and where we've come from, and what we stand for ... any mission would need that sympathy".

This comment would suggest that the indigenous Welsh were more aware of their distinct *ethnie* than recent arrivals who saw themselves as belonging to a mixed community. *Missio Dei* churches tended to express the perspective of the latter, not the former. In urban communities, and those with a population in flux, such an approach would be inclusive and generous. However, among static populations, and communities feeling under threat, such an approach might alienate and align the church with the incomers. Generally, *Missio Dei* churches were inclusive of all, ecumenical, and accommodating, minimising differences between peoples.

Adjusting to the Linguistic and Cultural Aspects
of Welsh Context

Missio Dei leaders described the linguistic and cultural patchwork of Wales as other *Approaches* had. In anglicised areas, where the Welsh language was neither spoken nor valued, their mission was shaped accordingly. They spoke of rugby as the primary Welsh identifier in these areas. However, none spoke of using cultural connections for mission, beyond a church celebration of St David's Day. In urban communities, the diversity of languages made the Welsh language, and its associated culture, a minority interest.

In areas where Welsh was a valued language in the community, they spoke of using Welsh hymns, bilingual projection, and even "phonetic Welsh at weddings and funerals for committal, welcome and blessing". Welsh cultural practices such as male voice choirs were mentioned, but were said to be used merely to "entertain the visitors", rather than for mission. Other churches took a more positive stance on the Welsh language, and saw the language as an opportunity to serve their community. They were aware of this significant part of their community that they were not connected to, and so sought to build bridges to serve them in some way.

> "Welsh is spoken widely, and children are taught in school, the young people speak Welsh... There are people out there who won't speak to you in English unless they have to, and there are one or two who find it really difficult to speak to you in English".

Such churches not only held occasional Welsh services, and used Welsh in their children's events, but also hosted a Welsh-medium preschool, did special events for a Welsh medium Junior School, and spoke of Welsh classes for learners. These activities represented the clearest examples of *Missio Dei* churches adjusting their mission to language and culture, simply for the benefit of the recipients. Involvement in these activities arose from an awareness of the need to "look after and treasure" their language, a cause that had always been a part of their "mission mind-set". This mission seemed to have no evangelistic interface at any point.

In contrast, for some leaders, the Welsh language was seen as a hindrance, and "Welsh speakers to be ignorant, because they exclude English speakers". In the following example, the reactions expressed demonstrate a decided hostility to Welsh and its associated culture:

> "They impose Welsh on the schools. I question the ethics of imposing a foreign language on English children that are coming down to study. Nobody dare breathe that because they will be seen as anti-Welsh ... The non-Welsh speakers are Welsh but a bit different. They're not regarded with full colours".

These comments suggest a community divided by language and culture. Even Welsh speakers admitted that, "The English speaker would see the Welshness as a closed shop really". Such a context is the opposite of a mixed diverse cosmopolitan urban community, for which *Missio Dei's* inclusive ecumenism was better suited.

Adjusting to the Social Aspects of Welsh Context

It has been shown that *Missio Dei* churches did mission in local communities, for the good of the communities, along with all those in the community who were willing to work with them, whether churches or secular bodies. In describing these communities, *Missio Dei* leaders made repeated references to "community", "family", and "belonging". The sense of strong community cohesion had been diminished by low local employment and outward migration, but *Missio Dei* churches desired to renew and enhance it. The variety of projects run by churches demonstrates the extent to which *Missio Dei* churches adjusted their mission to the particular social aspects of context. One leader encapsulated these adjustments:

> "We have a very defined catchment area of two estates on our doorstep, one of social housing, one of mature social housing. There is a high degree of need in both. ... We seek to listen to needs and make every contact a positive and relevant opportunity for God to be at work... The only way it is distinctly Welsh is in the level of need".

The church was working within a particular area, listening to what the needs were, and responding to those needs in practical ways, with others in the community. This represented the key elements of the *Approach* of *Missio Dei*. In some of the poorer communities, the churches and agencies to work with were very limited, but broad cooperation was practiced where possible:

> "Everybody knows everybody, and there are so few organisations that we have to partner with all organisations. We are the only church so we partner with the school, we partner with the council. It's just that everybody knows everybody. When you know ten community leaders you know everybody".

The churches were often providing services that the State were no longer able or willing to staff or fund:

> "There is an ongoing need for youth work provision as some of the council run youth clubs have stopped ... We are aware of the need to provide for all age groups and also provide a meeting and activities for the older generation. Local groups are also looking for hall space to rent at a reasonable rate, in light of council rental rates rising".

The scale of such need points to a potential weakness of the *Missio Dei Approach*. To sustain such provision, for the long term, would require a strong and growing local church to resource it financially and in terms of labour. With nearly 75% of *Missio Dei* churches either declining or growing only marginally, the long term feasibility of such social engagement must be in question. Mission separated from evangelism may be unsustainable.

Adjusting to the Political Aspects of Welsh Context

Leaders of churches with a *Missio Dei Approach* to mission were aware of the political history and challenges in Wales, but viewed them variously. Observations on the negative psychological legacy of Wales's political and economic past were made widely. For some *Missio Dei* leaders, especially in Welsh language churches, this was a living issue, with church members supportive of nationalist politics:

> "Their political awareness is very high, but their political involvement might be low...the *gorthrwm*[143]... a feeling of being hard-done (to) by the English, having to be on the defensive and having to make our point over and over and over again".

For leaders in more anglicised areas, there was considerably less sympathy:

> "Welsh people are aggrieved. Offa's Dyke might be there, but it didn't do much good. There's a Welsh desire for independence. I meet nationalists occasionally, and have it pushed in my face."

The sense of grievance and oppression, it was suggested, was due to a "crazy mixed up historic understanding of facts", which had led to a high level of prejudice, particularly against the English: "They see themselves as second class to England. Not necessarily to English people, it's not real, it's a perceived thing".

---

143 A Welsh word used to convey a sense of oppression.

Such contrasting attitudes meant that there was no consistent *Missio Dei Approach* to political issues. However, when involvement with the various political processes and bodies was considered, there was a high level of political engagement at all levels (Chart 47).

Concern for, and engagement with, the social and economic needs of their community had led to the highest level of lobbying of all the *Approaches* to mission.

> "We have a number of folk who are regularly in contact with their MP, and the way that some of the laws are changing in this country. We have had teaching on social justice and as part of that we do encourage folk to engage on political matters to local MPs, the Welsh Assembly, and the Assembly Government".

This awareness and involvement had led to an engagement in the political process, beyond that seen in the other *Approaches*. Churches worked with their local council and social services on community projects. Sometimes the links were very close indeed: "We know all the local councillors, they are part of the church and come into the café to have their meetings here". Another church had the chair of the County Council in the church, which meant that the church hosted the Civic Service. Another church had a local councillor and a parliamentary candidate within the congregation, and another had the local member of the National Assembly as a church member.

This level of political engagement, involvement and cooperation was part of the local church's mission to the community, not its evangelism. It represented a deliberate and active involvement in local and national politics in Wales, but without any consistent loyalty to one political party. Church members were elected officials of both *Plaid Cymru* and the Conservative party, which represented the polar opposites of Welsh politics.

Reflections on the *Missio Dei* Approach

Local churches in Wales, with a *Missio Dei Approach* to mission, accepted the view that God was doing the work of his kingdom in all aspects of society, and the churches had to participate, with all the other parties involved. The scope of this mission was wide and the needs considerable. Though agreeing with the mission, many traditional churches were unable to participate actively, because their structures and resources would not permit it. Newer churches, not tied to historic patterns of church and ministry, were more active in a wider range of mission activities. Some churches were still involved in evangelism at some level, though resources were spread between mission and evangelism, and mission was the highest priority. The absence of numerical growth, a muted message, and an ageing demographic in many of the churches, called into question whether mission of such a scope and variety was realistic and sustainable in the long term.

The Lausanne *Approach* to Mission

Since the rise of Theological Liberalism, and its social gospel, Evangelicals took a separate and opposing path. Despite their nineteenth century heritage, Evangelicals began to regard social action and involvement with suspicion. However, the Evangelical position began to change in the 1960s, with the Wheaton declaration, and the founding of the Lausanne movement in 1974. This movement contends for an integral mission, expressed in the Lausanne Covenant which states:

> "We affirm that God is both the Creator and Judge of all men. We therefore should share his concern for justice and reconciliation throughout human society and for the liberation of men from every kind of oppression. ... Although reconciliation with man is not reconciliation with God, nor is social action evangelism, nor political liberation salvation".[144]

The Covenant states that evangelism is central to the church's mission, but that there is also a requirement "to take the whole gospel to the whole world".[145] By "the whole gospel" the Lausanne movement means a response to human needs in the areas of justice, ecology and compassion, as well as personal salvation.[146]

John Stott, a prominent Evangelical Anglican, was one of the prime movers for Lausanne. He had previously been active in the gatherings of the World Council of Churches, looking for ecumenical agreement. He spoke of the conflict with Liberals and of his desire for reconciliation and synthesis, and some of his formulations and achievements reflect

---

144 Lausanne, "The Lausanne Covenant," Online: http://www.lausanne.org/covenant. ; Padilla, 'Historical,' in Chester, *Integral*, 46.
145 Lausanne, 'Covenant,' sec.6.
146 D. Birdsall and L. Brown, *The Cape Town Commitment: A Confession of Faith and a Call to Action* (Bodmin: Lausanne Movement, 2011), 27-29.

an attempt at accommodation.[147] The Lausanne Covenant makes a clear distinction between social action and evangelism, and Stott described the two elements, of the "great commandment" and the "great commission", as mission's dual aspects.[148] The movement's slogan, "The whole church taking the whole gospel to the whole world" represented a sea change for Evangelicals in the twentieth century, where social action was a separate "partner" with evangelism in holistic mission.[149] Wright speaks of mission going beyond evangelism, and not merely "whisking individuals off up to heaven".[150] The Lausanne understanding of mission is more restricted than *Missio Dei*, in that Christ's reign will only be expressed where Christ is confessed as Lord, so that the mission of God is not to be separated from the Church.[151] The Lausanne *Approach*, however, shows the unmistakeable influence of *Missio Dei* thinking, in which Trinitarian mission had become the Church's "royal charter". This is seen in the work of Tom Wright[152] and Chris Wright, where the partnership between evangelism and mission is likened to two blades of a pair of scissors.[153]

Stott distinguished between those who see social action as a "means", or a "manifestation", or as a "partner" to evangelism.[154] He and the Lausanne Movement favoured the latter, where the two elements are independent yet operate together. Lausanne thinking later developed to see the elements of social action and evangelism as equal and inseparable, speaking of a fusion between the two.[155]

147 J. R. W. Stott, *Christian Mission in the Modern World* (London: Falcon, 1975; repr., Downers Grove: Inter-Varsity, 2008), 12, 17, 20, 32.
148 Stott, *Mission*, 43-54.
149 Stott, *Mission*, 43-44.
150 C. J. H. Wright, *The Mission of God's People* (Grand Rapids: Zondervan, 2010), 73
151 Birdsall and Brown, *Cape Town Commitment*, 27-29.
152 N. T. Wright, *Surprised by Hope* (London: SPCK, 2007), 201-244, 277-283.
153 C. J. H. Wright, *The Mission of God* (Nottingham: Inter-Varsity, 2006), 316.
154 Stott, *Mission*, 41-45.
155 D. Burnett, *God's Mission: Healing the Nations* (Bromley: MARC Europe, 1986), 138; Padilla, *Mission Between the Times*, 1-25; C Van Gelder and D Zscheile J., *The Missional*

The Lausanne *Approach* represents a conscious refutation of Pietism's isolationism. Where Evangelicals had withdrawn into passivity, reacting to the emphasis of Theological Liberalism, they were "giving the field to the Social Gospel".[156] For Parry, Lausanne was a watershed for Evangelicals, and the social ethics of the Covenant were "now accepted as central by the evangelical mainstream".[157] Wright speaks of those that he still encountered, who "seem determined to turn the mission clock back to the first half of the twentieth century when evangelicals lost touch with their historical roots and embraced a view of mission as entirely or primarily evangelistic."[158] The issue of whether the mission of a local church should be "entirely or primarily evangelistic" represents something of a fault-line among evangelicals in Wales.

What the Questionnaire and Interviews showed

Charts 27 and 28 show that seventeen churches were identified as having a Lausanne *Approach* to local church mission. Of these, 41% were in the 5:2 category, which was a higher proportion than E1 churches (32%), but less than E2 churches (75%). Half of the churches with a Lausanne *Approach* were some of the largest congregations in Wales' cities and large towns, with Sunday attendances between 200 and 1,000. This may, in part, explain the number which were 5:2, as it is less of a challenge for a church in the hundreds to see five added in a decade and two in a single year, than for a church of a much smaller size. Also, the larger size of church may indicate that a church has to have a certain strength and scale to be able to

---

Church in Perspective: Mapping Trends and Shaping the Conversation (Grand Rapids: Baker Academic, 2011), 34.

156 R. M. Jones, *Crist a Chenedlaetholdeb* (Bridgend: Brintirion, 1998), 30, 41, 116-117.

157 R. Parry, "Evangelicalism and Ethics," in *The Futures of Evangelicalism* (ed. C. Bartholomew, R. Parry, and A. West; Leicester: Inter-Varsity, 2003), 165.

158 Wright, "Future Trends in Mission," in Bartholomew, Parry, and West, *Futures*, 162.

engage in varied social projects apart from evangelistic activities.

In terms of activities, the mission of Lausanne churches looked similar to E2 churches, being involved in *Foodbank*, debt relief (CAP), night-shelter, café and drop-in centres, community youth work and other services to the community. The difference from E2 engagement was that Lausanne churches were willing to provide services to the community for largely altruistic reasons, with only an indirect link to church meetings or to evangelistic programmes. It was hoped that involvement with one might lead to interest in the other. These included asylum support, teaching English as a foreign language, domestic classes for Muslim women, a centre for the elderly, dementia care and community youth clubs. Two churches were working, at the request of the local police, to draw youngsters off the streets where they were causing disruption. Another Lausanne church agreed to run a day centre for the elderly:

> "... the council approached to see we would take over [name] Street Centre, which is over half a mile away, senior citizens lunches Monday to Friday, so we entered into a contract with them for three years. ...we serve 20 people every day having a lunch who don't have anything to do with church really."

The church leader's analysis clearly reflected a Lausanne *Approach*: "I see mission and evangelism as two concentric circles. I see evangelism at the centre, and mission as something wider that links to the central theme." Such a distinction between "mission" and "evangelism" is illustrative of a Lausanne *Approach*. Social action was part of the church's mission, for its own sake, the two elements being independent, and yet operating together.

There was an underlying conviction, in Lausanne churches, that people needed to see the benefits brought by the churches in their community. Only then would evangelism have any relevance:

"I think the communication is through what we do, more than what we say. So that as a church we would endeavour to find ways to put flesh on that, through all the programs that we are involved in ... it is more an organic thing."

For one Lausanne leader, this had meant a fundamental change in how he viewed the ministry of the local church:

"I think we have been seeking to shift from the focus of trying to get people into "church" and moving towards trying to take Christ to the community. These are still early days for this shift in focus. We need to see an incarnational church where Christ is manifest in the community. Church will then shape around it rather than the other way round."

Lausanne churches looked similar to other Evangelical churches, but their understanding of the nature of their mission had changed their orientation as churches, and their effect on their communities. This trend is implied in the fact that Lausanne churches had a lower proportion of Church Related activities as the "most used" means of connecting to their communities (Chart 40).

This would reflect their intention to engage with society for society's sake, rather than as a means to draw society into the sphere of the church. This is further evidenced in the number of Lausanne churches doing Need and Youth related ministry (Chart 59), and especially in the churches that "most used" those connections (Chart 60). The churches did little Learning related mission to their communities, and no Lausanne church used the approach as "most used". This would suggest that, as Lausanne churches surveyed the needs of their communities, learning related needs were not seen as a high priority.

The charts 39-45, showing how the different *Approaches* to mission connected to their communities overall, show the same patterns. Lausanne churches, compared to the other *Approaches,* focussed more of their mission on families, the young and the needy, in preference to activities based around the church building, a café, or learning, where the felt needs of the community were less evident.

The Lausanne Message and Means of Communication

Lausanne leaders described their primary message as essentially evangelistic, but paralleled it with active social engagement:

- "There is a God, he is interested in you, loves you and we are here if you want to know more".

- "Jesus said I am the way the truth and the life. Such true life and true knowledge and true guidance in life is possible through knowing God revealed in Jesus Christ. Jesus said he had come to give his life and life in all its fullness".

- "They matter to God. I think that's where I would start".

- "The transforming love of Jesus for the community, [We are] a tribe of disciples who are passionate together in the Holy Spirit to share their fathers passion".

- "People need to know that God loves them, but on its own that doesn't mean a lot, so we are determined to love God and to love people, and to serve God and to serve people so our strapline is love in action. We want to take God's love and show it in practical ways".

- "We want them to observe it as well, God loves them and there is a better way to live. If you follow him you will find that better way".

When Lausanne churches were asked how they sought to communicate their message to their community (Chart 61), the responses showed that all groups of evangelistic means were used, and some approaches from the groups were used more than once. The variety of methods used was also shown in how people had responded to the message, leading them to join the church (Chart 62). However, when asked which approaches were used most (Chart 63), the Direct methods were less evident. Their use of Direct methods was less than other *Approaches* to mission, except for the Emergent churches which did not use them at all (Chart 36).

The number of Lausanne churches that had church services as one of the "most used" methods for communicating its message was lower than in Evangelistic churches (Chart 33), with only a third of these being 5:2 churches. This may be evidence that an intentional use of church services, in an attractional way, still has effectiveness in evangelism, or it may merely be a feature of larger churches, where the 5:2 criteria was easier to reach, and where a crowd attracts a crowd. Certainly, the responses did not demonstrate that smaller Lausanne churches achieved the same proportion of 5:2 growth.

The relatively low use of church services, and particularly the significantly low use of Direct means of evangelism, reflected the Lausanne emphasis on being part of the community, not a body that enters for evangelism and then withdraws. The proportion of 5:2 churches, within those with a Lausanne *Approach*, may also reflect a consequence of using a significant proportion of the church's resources for humanitarian mission rather than evangelism. For Evangelistic churches, communicating the message was the absolute priority in mission. Having a double emphasis would seem to affect the church's growth patterns, and could, eventually, affect the availability of people and resources to perform the mission, in that growth produces the needed resources for mission.

Adjusting to the Religious Aspects of Welsh Context

The Lausanne *Approach* to mission has been shown to involve a reorientation of the local church in relation to its ministry and mission. This change was a challenging task in traditional, and especially Welsh language, areas. One Welsh language minister spoke of the ministry and mission of his predecessor as being entirely pastoral, centred on church members and reaching out to, and through, their families. The current minister saw that effective mission, in the present and future, would have to be "outreach outside the church. This is the greatest challenge for my ministry in the future". Such transitions, however, could only be in areas of Wales where there were churches capable of such a change.

The situation in Wales, described by Lausanne leaders, was similar to the Evangelistic churches, but without any perception of positive opportunities in the old patterns. Because they tended to be larger, and situated in urban settings, where the traditional mores of Welsh society were less evident, the churches were contemporary and had made significant change in their ecclesiology. They saw no future for the traditional Welsh patterns of chapel life at all, but rather "our primary concern is to try to be church within the community and that is to get our people acting as Christians in a missional sense". Mission within Lausanne churches called for a fundamental change. Engagement with the community would begin a social transformation that would breed hope.

Adjusting to the Geographic Aspects of Welsh Context

Lausanne churches tended to be located in larger towns and cities, mostly in south Wales. Six were in the Valleys, six in Cardiff, and one each in Swansea, Bridgend, Llanelli and Haverfordwest. Four were in north Wales coastal towns, one in Wrexham, and one in mid Wales. None were in villages, and only in mid Wales was there a Lausanne church that was in a predominantly rural area. One church was Welsh-speaking. Therefore, their geographical spread was limited, and the type of communities served was almost exclusively urban or semi-urban.

However, Lausanne churches had the same awareness of the variety of local distinctives across Wales:

> "... a town that is more like a village. It's a community that is made up of various groups, almost tribal in their identity as (place) people or (place) people, and yet they are all passionately Welsh, identified with this community but they have a village mentality".

The Lausanne churches with the strongest sense of loyalty to locality, were in the south Wales Valleys. Leaders in the Valleys communities had the same high sense of localism described by the Evangelistic church leaders. One leader described the context graphically:

> "I am a man of the Rhondda before I'm a man of Wales, almost. It is that Valleys feeling, some of the things that happen in the Rhondda you wouldn't see in some of the bigger cities for sure. Sometimes that colloquialism is almost profound. I betray my village of Treherbert by playing rugby for Treorchy, a mile down the road!... When it's Treorchy against Pontypridd I'd be fully behind Treorchy. When it's Pontypridd against Cardiff then I'll be behind Pontypridd! When it's Wales against England, it's Wales."

This church ran *Foodbank*, a café, CAP and other community initiatives to serve its immediate constituency.

The larger urban and semi-urban communities, that had seen higher levels of inward and outward migration, had a less evident loyalty to place. However, an awareness of a village mentality still remained. One city church spoke of attitudes to locality in a pejorative way: "It's something to do with feeling slightly marginalised, feeling that there is a rootedness, a history, about where you come from... I think there can be a small-mindedness, parochialism ...". This church had worked extensively with the local authority to support the marginalised and mentally challenged, as a direct response to the local conditions they observed.

A city centre church, with a large student and immigrant population in its adjacent community, was challenged by the fact that the majority of those attending drove in from the suburbs. The leader commented that the church building was in its locality for a reason, and decided to define its own "square mile" for mission purposes. They got involved in *Foodbank*, a provision for the homeless, a day centre for the elderly, two English classes catering for up to 80 Muslim background people, a sewing and cooking class for Muslim women, community fun days, regeneration days of garden weeding or car-washing, and an international's work for 70 to 80 students of different nationalities. This was done for holistic reasons, aware that it was bridge-building to a community when, previously, the only contact was "that we parked our cars outside their houses which was very annoying too. It was a very negative association". The church had created its own local identity, and served the community within it.

Lausanne churches, though mostly within urban communities, still recognised a measure of localism present in their communities: "There is an affinity with the *milltir sgwar*, your own patch, a love towards the place where you grow up, but your primary identity is Welsh". This was a feature of Welsh contexts that Lausanne churches seemed to have capitalised on, in that it gave a defined area, a particular people, and set of needs to respond to.

Adjusting to the Ethnic Aspects of Welsh Context

Lausanne is an international movement that encourages cooperation between churches in different nations, and celebrates national diversity. For Lausanne churches, the presence of different cultures, languages, traditions and approaches to mission, internationally and the local church, is desirable, and is seen as a particular feature and strength of the Christian Church. This may, in part, explain why Lausanne churches tended to be located in larger towns, and along the border with England, where there was greater population diversity and movement.

> "It's not just that they speak English, a sizeable proportion of the people are English. I have never led a church in Wales, I've only led a church in Cardiff. I do believe that Cardiff, and especially parts of Cardiff, is unique. I think that (place name) is essentially English."

This comment, by a leader born in a west Wales valley, showed that parts of the urban areas of Wales were cosmopolitan to such an extent, that they could be considered so English as to be not a part of Wales at all.

Leaders spoke of the different nationalities in their churches and the communities they were seeking to reach and serve:

> "...many people speak various overseas languages as speak Welsh in our church, showing its diversity... outside the church our city is supposedly a city of refuge for refugees, and there are many various languages spoken on the streets".

154

The classes for Muslim women, described earlier, illustrate this ethnic diversity and one church's missional response to it. However, those on the Welsh / English border, said that there was no one single ethnic identity: "We are in some senses a bit like borderland country we not sure fully of our identity". Therefore, the mission of the churches in such areas made little application to a Welsh ethnicity.

In the Valleys, where recent inward migration had been limited and where people of a different ethnicity were less than 1% of the population, there was a degree of homogeneity. This generated a loyalty to a sense of tribe, but also an ongoing hostility to those who were different:

> "Approximately 0.5 % of the population are from an ethnic minority which is far lower than Wales as a whole – however, racial harassment particularly from the youngsters and targeting local shopkeepers and takeaway staff is occasionally a problem."

The leaders of Lausanne churches sought to identify with, be a part of, and represent that distinct Valleys identity. In the Valleys, they tended to serve the majority, not the minorities.

Adjusting to the Linguistic and Cultural Aspects of Welsh Context

One Lausanne church in Gwynedd was Welsh-speaking only, and its minister active in promoting and defending the Welsh language. This leader contended that people needed to hear and respond to Christian truth in their heart language:

> "The best way to reach and evangelize Welsh speakers is through Welsh churches. I have non-Christian friends who would never listen to the

155

message of the gospel in English because they associate the English language as a foreign language..."

The church's mission, therefore, was to a specific language group, and contextualised to this language and its non-English culture. This position on language, however, was exceptional in Lausanne churches. As stated earlier, Lausanne, as an international movement, sees the church as a place of racial integration and acceptance, not exclusion. Lindsay Brown, the International Director of the Lausanne Movement, is a Welshman from Merthyr Tydfil, in the anglicised south Wales Valleys. When speaking at the Evangelical Movement of Wales English Conference in August 2012, he stated a Lausanne position, provoking some controversy among Welsh speakers. He spoke of his pride in his Welsh roots and identity, but said that mono-ethnic and mono-cultural churches lost the "compulsive attractiveness" seen in the New Testament Churches. These transcended ethnic divisions, rather than tempering and weakening their witness through limiting themselves to a single ethnie. These contrasting attitudes will be considered in Section Three.

A more common approach by Lausanne churches would be to do parts of services, publicity, and small group activity through the medium of Welsh, whilst making English the predominant language of the church. Traditional Welsh hymns and tunes would be incorporated within worship, but there would be no plans to establish a Welsh language church, or to encourage Welsh speakers to attend one. Another church was keen to identify itself as bilingual, and for people to have a Welsh church experience when they attended. They were seeking to help people, who had moved into Wales from other places, to incorporate into Wales and Welshness. They were less orientated to building a bridge to reach and serve Welsh speakers in the community. Welsh-speaking Christians were to be part of English-speaking congregations that served communities multi-lingually and multi-culturally.

In south Wales there was some use of traditional culture, such as choral singing, to connect with the community, but the culture in their areas was more associated with rugby, in that people "might never have been to a game, but they are a rugby fan". Other modern expressions of Welshness, such as the National Assembly and contemporary Welsh music, were also valued. The traditional icons of Welshness, such as language and *eisteddfodau*, had become dated and passé: "The *eisteddfod* which was a bit sad and not exciting... Culture has changed, the Cool Cymru movement... The Welsh government, and having that identity, has helped". Instead of identifying with the Welsh language and traditional culture, this church ran a café for parents and children, from Welsh and English schools.

Lausanne churches, therefore, adjusted to the Welsh language and cultural traditions as appropriate to their context. However, their largely urban and English language contexts, with the exception of the one Welsh language church, meant that a multi-cultural approach, using English as the *Lingua Franca,* predominated.

Adjusting to the Social Aspects of Welsh Context

Like E2 churches, Lausanne churches sought to be actively involved in their communities. They differed, however, in that they were willing to be involved whether or not there was an obvious evangelistic opportunity for their message. In several cases, they actually surveyed the community to identify the priority needs, or joined with what was already happening, or approached the local council to ask what was needed. As a result the local authorities, and the police, came back to the churches looking for partnership.

"We have built on activities that are already taking place in the community, for example, schools and youth work, ladies craft club. (Place) has a very strong community feel and so we built other activities around community, for example opening a community café. There is also a strong emphasis on family so we organised an annual family fun night".

The variety of activities provided in the community by Lausanne churches, as noted above, was very extensive. The conviction that churches were to be involved in the communities around them, for the benefit of those communities, had led to practical results. The success of these activities was measured in the positive changes in society: the declining youth violence in the streets, improving results in schools, raising morale in the community, and providing employment. Gains for the church itself were a hoped for consequence, but not a condition. The motivation for this was compassion not evangelism. The starting point was said to be Jesus' command to give a cup of water in his name, and that they would help people because they, and God, loved them. If this did not lead to interest in their message or church, or even a rejection of both, "we would still stay with them".

Adjusting to the Political Aspects of Welsh Context

The Lausanne declaration encouraged churches to take an active role in issues of justice, ecology and compassion as part of God's mission to God's world. Such an engagement inevitably involved engagement in the political sphere. The responses recorded by the different *Approaches* to mission demonstrate this involvement by Lausanne churches, at a local if not a national level (Chart 47). The 100% engagement with local government reflected the high level of cooperation in social projects between such churches and local authorities. Not only did these churches seek to alleviate need, but also to "teach a pride in our community and nationhood", and "to raise aspiration in the community".

Labourism was seen to have failed to remedy the situation, but one leader saw current government policy as an opportunity for the churches to bring real change:

> "David Cameron says austerity is here to stay, we have to do more with less, then I think it's an opportunity for church to embed itself more in providing some of the services that are currently statutory services."

This leader spoke of the opportunity being an ongoing challenge to the church to be increasingly involved, and to diversify in their activities, "in an incarnational way". This would involve continuing change for the church, to be less of a "professional attraction" and "more earthling community ... and that to give rise to all sorts of new ways of being and doing church". The church was already running a community café, dementia care and *Foodbank*.

Another significant engagement within the political sphere was the action of members of the Welsh language Lausanne church in the defence of the Welsh language. Members of this church had been active in the work of *Cymdeithas yr Iaith Gymraeg* / Welsh Language Society, formed in 1962 and modelled on the civil rights movement in the United States. They sought to defend and promote the use of the language in Wales, using non-violent direct action and civil disobedience to protest and petition for equal rights for the language. For Menna Machreth, a member of one of the Lausanne churches, such activities were her Christian duty:

> "After becoming a Christian, I didn't stop protesting, but gradually I came to understand how my campaigning couldn't be a self-centred or self-righteous act. Christ has redeemed me on the Cross, but He doesn't want to stop there

– he wants His justice to go throughout the world. ...my identity in Christ reinforced the identity God has given me on Earth, as part of a group of people. God has redeemed me in my Welshness".[159]

She claimed that the non-violent approach of the Society had been shaped by these Christian principles, an approach that meant:

"...no fist violence, no verbal violence, and no heart violence ...As Christians within the movement, we must act out of love at all times and must remember to love all the people we're involved with".

Unlike Evangelistic churches, which did not see evangelistic opportunities in political engagement, Machreth had come to faith through contact with Christians engaged in the same political activity, and saw her involvement as part of her testimony as a Christian. When speaking at the Lausanne Conference in Cape Town in 2010, she said;

"I have a great opportunity to share the gospel when they ask me why I campaign for the Welsh language. Before speaking at an event or going into a meeting with politicians, I pray for wisdom, strength and to be a witness to Him and God has been faithful and has blessed me in these situations as a campaigner."[160]

This example illustrates a fundamental difference between an Evangelistic and a Lausanne *Approach* to mission, in relation to political engagement. A Lausanne *Approach* saw contending for justice and individual rights as part of its mission, and part of the church's message of good news. Christians had not only been involved in political activity, but had sought to shape how that activity was conducted.

---

159 M. Machreth, "Ethnicity in the Mission of God," Online: HTTP://CONVERSATION. LAUSANNE.ORG/EN/CONVERSATIONS/DETAIL/11211#.VACFTVLDWSO .
160 Machreth, "Ethnicity," n.p.

Reflections on the Lausanne *Approach*

The message of Lausanne churches was similar to Evangelistic churches in their evangelism, and their mission was similar to E2 churches in their involvement in community. However, they had a significant extra motivation in their conviction that the mission of God, through the local church, included aspects of justice, ecology and compassion, as well as proclamation. This had led to a variety of social projects, done for the benefit of those who received them, albeit hoping for an indirect evangelistic connection. However, the urban context of Lausanne churches, and their larger size, raised a question as to whether such an approach to mission was feasible in smaller, rural situations. Also, the proportion of Lausanne churches that were 5:2 raised the possibility that the energy and resources put into mission, which was not directly evangelistic, was diverting these churches, at least in part, from its other central purpose.

The Emergent *Approach* to Mission

The Emerging Church movement,[161] or conversation as it is sometimes called, is a response to the developing post-modernity of the West.[162] Knowledge in post-modernity is seen as relative, contextual and affected by emotions, aesthetics and heritage, with no over-arching big picture. Therefore, Emergent leaders suggest that a "missional ecclesiology in a post-modern context needs to reflect the organic nature of the emerging context".

The members and leaders of Emergent churches came mostly from churches with an Evangelistic emphasis, adopting the *Missio Dei* agenda of social engagement, and, in some cases tended to the universalism and inclusivity of theological Liberalism. Brian McLaren, one of the best known and most articulate advocates of the Emerging Conversation, embraces this complexity by describing himself as:

"a missional + evangelical + post/protestant +liberal/conservative + mystic/ poet + biblical + charismatic/contemplative + fundamentalist/Calvinist + Anabaptist/anglican + Methodist + catholic + green + incarnational + depressed-yet-hopeful + emergent + unfinished CHRISTIAN".[163]

Emergent thinkers have tended to avoid sharp definitions of Christian conversion, and any sense of exclusivity, preferring inclusivity.[164] They

---

161 The terms "Emerging" and "Emergent" are used synonymously in this study. Attempts to distinguish their use have have been undermined by the lack of definition within the movement. In Wales no difference was evident in their use.

162 D. Kimball, *The Emerging Church: Vintage Christianity for New Generations* (Grand Rapids: Zondervan, 2003), 14.

163 B McLaren, *A Generous Orthodoxy* (Grand Rapids: Zondervan, 2004), title page.

164 E. Gibbs and R. K. Bolger, *Emerging Churches* (Grand Rapids: Baker Academic, 2005), 123, 132-134, 220; McLaren, *Generous*, 213; R. Bell, *Love Wins* (London: Collins, 2011), 97, 98, 107, 109.

reflect the influence of *Missio Dei* thinking, and freely acknowledge their indebtedness to Newbigin, Bosch and N. T. Wright.[165]

By the first decade of the twenty-first century, leaders and churches in Wales were adopting an Emergent *Approach* to mission. At the start of the new millennium, the new movement was viewed positively, as pointing to a hopeful way forward for declining congregations. In 2005, Gibbs and Bolger published their comprehensive review of the Emerging Church movement, with three examples from Wales: Linden fellowship in Swansea,[166] New Duffryn Community Church, Newport,[167] and Zac's Place, Swansea.[168] These were seen as encouraging and ground breaking examples of the new trends. In the preface to the second edition of his review of Christianity in the twentieth century, Morgan also mentions Zac's Place, Solace (a gathering in a Cardiff nightclub), "and similar endeavours".[169] These examples were all in urban, English speaking areas of south Wales, but hopes were raised that they represented a new beginning that could be replicated in other areas, contexts and cultures within Wales.

What the Questionnaire and Interviews showed

Charts 27 and 28 show that only four churches could be identified as having an Emergent *Approach* to local church mission, and one of these was in the 5:2 category. These responses were supplemented by other churches mentioned in print, and others who did not complete the questionnaire,

---

165 McLaren, *Generous*, 17, 115, 118, 288, 303; Gibbs and Bolger, *Emerging*, 26, 48-54, 59, 303-311.
166 Gibbs and Bolger, *Emerging*, 107, 121-122, 232, 280.
167 Gibbs and Bolger, *Emerging*, 53, 310-311.
168 Gibbs and Bolger, *Emerging*, 309.
169 Morgan, *Span, 2011*, xv.

but were willing to be interviewed. The following comments on this *Approach*, therefore, are based on a small sample.

The limited number of Emergent churches in Wales was the result of a number of factors. Firstly, by the end of the first decade of the twenty-first century, the Emergent movement had faltered, and not increased in number. It was unclear which, "similar endeavours" Morgan had in mind, but the numbers were small, and those mentioned were struggling or no longer functioning. New Duffryn Community Church continued as a Church in Wales partnership on a needy council estate in Newport, known as "The Lab". Zac's Place, known as "A Church for Ragamuffins" has developed as a centre supporting the homeless and most vulnerable in society, and Solace closed down. Its members were re-formed as a missional community in a Cardiff arts centre.

Secondly, the edges were blurred between this and other *Approaches*, especially *Missio Dei*, where both *Approaches* were ecumenical in nature and strongly influenced by Newbigin's work. Some churches that self-identified as Lausanne were very close to Emergent in that the evangelistic elements in their mission, were presented in a visual not vocal way. One of the churches mentioned earlier by Gibbs and Bolger, in interview, actually identified themselves as Lausanne in approach, even though many of their mission methods were Emergent.

Thirdly, the Emergent movement, and its expression of mission, morphed into missional initiatives that were programmes and expressions of existing churches. The *Fresh Expressions* movement operates mostly within existing Anglican and Nonconformist denominations, and the Methodist Church listed *Messy Church*, cafés, youth events and missional cells as their Welsh expressions. Thus, the demise of the Emergent *Approach* may have been a result of its own success, in that others had taken over their methods, to the potential benefit of all.[170] Its emphasis on small missional communities, embedded within areas of need, is a case in point, and this will be considered further in Section Three.

Churches with an Emergent *Approach* to mission sought to establish communities of Christians within the society they were seeking to reach. Theirs was a non-institutional model, demonstrating good news by serving. They avoided rigid definitions on church structure, doctrine and discipleship, seeking to be flexible and adaptive to a particular context in post-modern and post-Christendom Wales. They looked for what God was doing in the place being served: "I don't take God into somewhere, but find him where he is and join him", or "Rather than sucking things into serving the church, our focus is to be out and about being church". Emerging churches looked for a transformation of the society around them, through being part of that society and serving it.

The members of Emergent churches sought to be embedded within their local community, in its activities, relationships and needs. Mission had to be "incarnational", where there was a long term commitment to be in, and part of, the local community: "To do that we have to be here and model it". This *Approach* to mission involved serving the community for its overall good. The impact of service on the community was understood as a way to demonstrate the kingdom of God through practical expressions of the love of God.

> "Much of our work has a Kingdom emphasis rather than Church focus (both missional and incarnational). Demonstrating hope through action amongst people who feel hopeless".

---

170 One example of another approach affirming the Emergent contribution is found in the Liberal network *Cristnogaeth21*'s conference in 2010, where the Emergent *Approach* was highlighted, and one of its leaders contributed. T. Ifan, "Neges Misol Mai 2010," Online: http://www.cristnogaeth21.org/?p=104#more-'.

This emphasis is seen in the community connections of Emergent churches. The charts, which compare Emergent churches' overall connections to their communities (Charts 39 to 45), show the comparatively low use of multiple Church related activities, with Café, Need, Youth and Learning approaches comparatively high.

However, when compared to "most used" responses (Chart 64), Café, Family and Learning approaches did not register, suggesting that their use was very occasional. On the other hand, the use of Need and Youth in "most used" were higher than all other *Approaches*. Emergent churches used Church activities, but their primary mission was to youth and children, and social needs, in their community.

For new churches, which began with an Emergent *Approach*, the initial challenges involved being accepted in the community they wished to serve. However, for existing churches, which had transitioned to an Emergent model, the challenges related to the expectations of existing members.

> "I think we have been seeking to shift from the focus of trying to get people into "church" and moving towards trying to take Christ to the community. These are still early days for this shift in focus".

For some churches, this involved the loss of existing members in a painful transition.

The Emergent mission, however, was not about the Church, but transforming the wider community. The ethos was "to love God and people and to play their part in making the world a better place ... a prosperous and safe place in which to live", being a church in the world, constantly interacting with people.

The Emergent Message and Means of Communication

This expression of love was to be unconditional and inclusive, and in no way dependant on whether someone came to the church or believed what the church believed. For that reason, a direct evangelistic message was avoided. God was seen to love people exactly as they are, and people were on a journey towards him.

- "The message is that God loves people, and we can't say we love God and not love people. Everybody can change. Everybody can change ... What we do in the building does reflect the message, the message of inclusion, of empowerment of people, of loving people and wanting people to live their best life. You know, personally, I see that in Jesus, he wanted people to live their best life that they could".

- "The church's vision statement is to reach the local community with the love of Christ. To be a God centred community, reaching the people with the love of Christ and bringing hope where there is hopelessness. God is a God who cares for them, can be trusted in their everyday lives and wants a relationship with them".

- "Love your lord God with all your heart mind and strength, with the emphasis on loving God with all your heart ... this is among people who are medicated up to the eyeballs, broken-hearted, suicidal thoughts. Anything we say will only be received if it's matched by something done".

- "That God loves you exactly as you are, and you don't have to become anything before you can know that love... I think people can see very quickly through an agenda, even if it's the best intended agenda in the world. Acceptance is incredibly important...

we emphasise the journey metaphor a lot, and where I am on that journey is different to where you are on your journey. It's not for me to look and say that you are not far enough on your journey... I feel very uncomfortable about making judgement calls about other people".

This was a message that emphasised personal improvement and change, helping people on their spiritual journey. It did not emphasise faith in the death and resurrection of Jesus as the means to that change, which may explain why those who were impressed by their service did not necessarily share in their faith. Murray's cautionary note is salutary: "Some emerging churches avoid evangelism altogether. And yet ... Without evangelism there will be no church after Christendom, nor any way of sustaining other dimensions of mission".[171]

As has been explained earlier, the role of friendship and community involvement were seen as an important part of mission. However, the questionnaire responses show that this was for the sake of community connection, and not evangelism.

> "As we cast our vision, we realised that God was changing our focus away from event orientated evangelism to process orientated service".

Emergent churches made little use of Relational or Direct approaches to communicating their message (Chart 65), especially the "most used" which shows regular, not occasional use (Chart 66). They did use "Services", but at the lowest rate of all the *Approaches* in both the overall use (Chart 32) and of the methods "most used" (Chart 33).

When asked about the particular means of communicating the message,

---

171 Murray, *Church After Christendom*, 163.

these churches seemed to focus on the impact of the actual activity, without necessarily any deliberate communication of a verbal message. One leader, when asked about evangelistic activity, replied, "Drama, debate (most used), art & craft". The place of debate, where various views were shared and considered, was central to another church's "Spirituality Café", held monthly, as an opportunity for "spiritual seekers", from an eclectic background, to share about their spiritual journey. This was followed by discussion where, "We have all sorts there, but everyone feels safe, and there's no pressure". The venues used were to be non-religious, such as a pub, or ideally, "a pub that is owned and run by the community... The church taking over bowling alleys, cafés, clubs". The message was communicated by deeds, as a way of helping individuals change, not as evangelism aimed at adding them to the local church:

> "Throughout the transitional process we encouraged the congregation to see the community not as a potential place for church growth but as a place where we are called to enter with listening love".

When asked how people had come to faith, and been added to the church, Emergent churches still showed some reliance on church activities (Chart 67). Evangelistic conversations and courses, and church services, were effective, at least with some. The importance of work with youth and children followed the same patterns as other *Approaches*, but the use of "Mission" was notable. Emergent churches used the term "mission" exclusively of its community activity, and never as a week-long evangelistic enterprise as organised by some Evangelistic churches.

For Emergent churches mission involved serving the community in practical ways, in order to transform the community into a better place to live, something that was not only seen as possible, "but is our very reason to exist".

Adjusting to the Religious Aspects of Welsh Context

One Emergent leader described their challenges as contextual, not circumstantial:

> "There is a movement, there is a groundswell of something that is happening in Britain through the Emerging Church and the missional communities, and in Wales we seem to be missing out somehow … ".

It was felt that the Welsh context was not responsive to such new movements. Though Emergent congregations seemed effective in other parts of the United Kingdom, and beyond, resistance was encountered in Wales. This was variously accounted for by the negative legacy of the chapel tradition, a resistance to change and new ideas, and loyalty to accepted forms:

> "There is something almost rooted in Welshness, a stubbornness, a refusal to want to change, or move on … Welsh people almost feel they are letting themselves down if they admit that how they have always done things isn't working".

The traditional models were no longer working, and, therefore, should be abandoned: "When the horse is dead, dismount". Another foresaw only small missional communities existing in the future, with only a few traditional churches left, "pockets of resistance, fortress outpost is of the old ways... Island fortresses in a sea of people who don't care". It was for this reason that Emergent leaders rejected all traditional forms as doomed and ineffective. The Welsh people were not opposed to Jesus *per se*, but to the religious system that represented him.

> "In this village over 80% on the census said that they were Christians. I think that is staggering. 80%, so people are not against God, people are against the institutional Church and what it has become".

Emergent leaders expected the era of Nonconformist chapels and traditions to come to an imminent end, and so were preparing new, flexible structures, that would give a contemporary representation and relevance to the Christian faith: "I don't feel disheartened that the church will die out.... I think it will be hard to define how this thing will look". It was acknowledged that the hope of people responding to God's love, through seeing love expressed, gave no guarantee of future attendance: "Whether or not that means that they come here on Sunday, I don't know if that's what will happen. It may well happen, but I think the influence of the love of God to pervade this village, that is my vision".

The problem for Emergent churches was that the people of Wales were not yet ready for the change. Emergent churches had struggled to multiply, and their dream of community transformation remained a dream. The legacy and memory of chapel tradition meant that Welsh communities were not ready for the new approach.

Adjusting to the Geographic Aspects of Welsh Context

Emergent churches in Wales were working in some of the most deprived housing communities in the cities and post-industrial Valleys. The work was focussed on the small communities they were serving, and the embedded nature of their mission showed a high level of adjustment to place, locality and community boundaries. They did not attempt to work across wide areas. The small cellular nature of all but one of the churches meant that they could be easily multiplied to serve other local communities. Their service in communities was adjusted to that community, and its history, as they sought to be contextual.

Adjusting to the Ethnic Aspects of Welsh Context

The Emergent churches that responded to the Survey and the interviews were in south Wales in areas that had seen periods of significant inward migration. Therefore, no mention was made of a primordial Welshness, but there was an awareness of a Welsh *ethnie* derived from history. A sense of historical rootedness lay behind an identification with Celtic models of spirituality and community. Similarly, the Emergent churches serving communities in the post-industrial Valleys were also aware of an identity based on industrial history and its legacy. One church set out to respond in its mission to the negative legacy of mine closures, poverty and unemployment. They sought to create an awareness of what was good in their community through looking at their potential instead of the need. They ran a family fun day every year, with a photographic competition of places in the area: "It is just a way of showing that they live in a really beautiful place. Don't keep knocking it". The sense of local community in the Valleys was something that small Emergent churches could become a part of, thus identifying with the local expression of Welshness: "People feel very strongly Welsh ... It is very kind of tribal ... There is a sense of being the underdog". These observations were no different from those of other *Approaches* to mission, but the Emergent churches' willingness to embed within a community meant that their identification with those communities was very high.

Adjusting to the Linguistic and Cultural Aspects of Welsh Context

All the Emergent churches were in south Wales English language areas. A small Welsh-speaking community in north Wales survived only briefly, closing before the *Waleswide* Survey was conducted. The radical and non-traditional forms of Emergent churches were viewed with suspicion in communities that still valued the Welsh chapel tradition as part of their inherited culture, even if they no longer attended. As seen earlier, Emergent churches were regarded as alien, as English, or as a threatening change.

Emergent leaders reflected some of the hostility to the Welsh language expressed in the Valleys. They were embedded in communities that were proud of their own Welshness and traditions, but these cultural traditions were not shaped by language. The culture of Valley communities was expressed though rugby and its attendant culture: "There's a big sporting element in the village, rugby is a very Welsh thing. ... Another Welsh thing, the community pub, for this village anyway has played a huge part". Emergent churches were part of such communities, except for one, which was meeting in an art gallery and connected with an urban artistic culture. Adjustments to language and culture, therefore, were within these small urban communities, and reflected their preferences. The attitudes to Welsh language and culture, described above, would create significant resistance outside urban and anglicised areas. Emergent churches struggled with the linguistic and cultural aspects of Welsh contexts, issues which they had not found to be a problem in other nations in the UK.

Adjusting to the Social Aspects of Welsh Context

Being located within needy communities, Emergent churches were very conscious of their social context, especially those in the post-industrial Valleys. They commented on the "community feel" of such areas, and sought to adjust to it.

"...even though we live in a day when communities tend to be fragmented and there are family breakdowns, here there is a real identity of family and identity of community. You might call it tribal, but there is still that feel here. ... People already have a very strong set of relationships".

The Emergent churches connected to the patterns of these relationships by seeking to "step into the community and immerse ourselves as much as we can into the community by getting involved in things that are already happening. By attempting to do things that continue that community feel". By living within the communities, they were accessing existing interrelated networks. They were seeking to model a different lifestyle: "you don't have to go and get smashed every weekend, there is another way of loving each other". The areas of involvement were described as "maintaining the graveyard (the neglect of which was identified as distressing to local residents)", food distribution, home refurbishment, craft club, furniture recycling, a gym for health and fitness, IT, needlework and language courses, and a youth worker working as a rugby coach for the local team.

There can be no doubt that such a range of social provision, from a small number of local communities, is impressive. Operating from within communities, as part of the community, in a small and flexible cell, meant that adjustment to urban and Valley contexts was effective. Whether such groups would be sustainable in the long term, or how such a model would apply to more prosperous, rural, or traditional Welsh language communities is an open question, as the number of such churches is declining.

Adjusting to the Political Aspects of Welsh Context

One of the Emergent churches that closed had been involved in protests against sweatshops, modern day slavery and people trafficking. They organised city-centre stunts, including a protest outside Primark, and a mock slave auction outside a library. Another leader, in the Valleys, had been a Labour Party activist, but an attempt to impose a candidate locally led to him to change to non-political action. Another leader had offered to stand as a candidate for the local council, but was resisted because they were not a Labour Party member.

Compared to other *Approaches* to mission, Emergent churches were most involved at the local level, campaigning for the needs of their community (Chart 47). Whether such political action, however, was in any way an adjustment to the distinctives of the Welsh political context, is questionable. Churches in other distinct national contexts, especially in areas of social deprivation, could well be politically active in exactly the same way. The absence in their communities of political aspirations linked to language, culture and national independence, meant that there was less of a distinctly Welsh political context to adjust to.

Reflections on the Emergent *Approach*

By being embedded in local communities, the Emergent churches demonstrated a high level of contextualisation to the localism, identity, and social needs of their communities. Their approach to mission demonstrated a high level of commitment to the transformation of those communities. However, the pattern of mission seemed to run contrary to the religious context of Wales, even in its most anglicised and secular areas. The covert nature of their message meant that few were added to their number from those communities. Mission without an urgent message, once again, did not replenish the church doing the mission. As a result the churches did not multiply or spread, and the hopes of a movement to transform the church / mission landscape at the start of the millennium had been all but exhausted by the end of the decade. Wales was not ready, or was not good ground, for the seed of an Emergent *Approach* to mission.

Section Three:

A New Mission: Where do we go from here?

This Section will consider the prospects for churches in Wales in the next decade. We will consider the lessons to be drawn from the adjustments made to the differing *Aspects* of Welsh contexts by the various *Approaches* to mission, and reflect on a number of challenging issues that have been raised. Some of the answers arise naturally out of the analysis of the findings from the questionnaire and the interviews, but these will be clarified and developed by the findings of the *Soundings* held in 2015. The *Soundings* were sixteen regional gatherings, two in Welsh, which invited perspectives on the current state of churches in their area, how the situation is likely to develop over the next decade, and what steps need to be taken now in order to prepare adequately for the challenges to be faced. The perspectives offered are confirming, but also suggest further steps that churches and groups of churches might need to consider taking.

The differing effectiveness of the six *Approaches* suggests things to avoid as well as to adopt, but any 'good practice' learned will have to be calibrated to the specific features of a local context. Whether effective mission is seen, primarily, in terms of the local church's influence on its community, or its evangelistic efforts that could secure its own survival and growth, the ability to contextualise will be critical. Robinson puts the issue clearly:

> "... the answer to the question of the decline of the church does not lie in a particular programme or model of the church. Instead we have to learn how to do mission – in our cultural context – deeply contextualized and profoundly local... the willingness to connect with and to serve at a deep level the communities in which they are located".[172]

---

172 M. Robinson, "Post Christian and Post Secular Europe," Online: http://www. eurochurch.net/news/articles/post-christian-and-post-secular-europe.php.

Religious:
The Way We Do Church

The Welsh religious context at the beginning of the twenty-first century, in the views of writers (Section One) and local church leaders (Section Two), is unambiguous. Wales is no longer a land of chapel-goers, and the churches do not have the strength, influence, or status that they once had. Religion is increasingly marginalised in a consumerist and individualistic culture. According to Chambers and Thompson, "pervasive secularisation has bitten deeper and harder in Wales".[173] Descriptions of local indifference, scepticism, and even hostility, confirmed the existence of a chasm between traditional chapel culture and contemporary Wales.

The traditional churches were often existing like private clubs, without even a notice board to invite or inform potential visitors. If visitors did enter, they would experience esoteric and inaccessible worship from a former age, possibly in an unfamiliar language. The religious realities of Welsh society have changed, and many churches have not changed with them. The mission of the churches has been largely centripetal or attractional in nature, relying on invitation, obligation, and family loyalties to draw the wider community into its activities. A reluctance, or inability, to adjust to these changed religious realities has led to the near collapse of the historic denominations.

If local churches are not seen as contemporary and relevant, they will be viewed as a relic of a bygone age. Change is the price to pay for survival:

---

173 P. Chambers and A. Thompson, "Coming to Terms with the Past: Religion and Identity in Wales," *Social Compass* 53 (3 2005): 338.

Sounding Sense

In describing the current state of traditional churches the leaders were very frank:

"There is a distant memory, a sentiment of chapel, but if you peel away the surface there is a resentment. There is no love for it...There is an anger... denominations and clericalism are dead ... Chapel-ness is the curse of Wales... The only thing we've got going for us in Wales is that we've fallen off the cliff first ... People have started to see that we can't continue as we are". However, twelve of the *Soundings* had also seen real encouragements, and said things like, *"I am rather hoping that in ten years an awful lot of doors shut really... they need to close. We need to get off our backsides and do something. If chapels were not there, there would be an opportunity to do something different... The gospel light will shine brighter in 10 years' time"*.

"What we have now is a vibrant church that works with the community, and works with real people. We don't want to be sat down watching black-and-white movies forever, and we don't want church to be that way either, so we have moved on, to a generation that has moved on."

The term "missional", describes holistic mission, where church, evangelism and social action are variously combined. The six *Approaches* to mission use the term, but do so differently, reflecting their particular emphases. What is affirmed by all, is that the post-Christendom era calls for an outward, not inward, expression of mission. The relatively higher growth in E2 and Lausanne churches demonstrated the brighter prospects for a church's mission when it is centrifugal, outreaching, evangelistic, and serving its wider community. The achievements of such *Approaches* are in contrast to other *Approaches*, where mission is more traditional and attractional.

Evangelism as a Component of Mission

E1, E2 and Lausanne churches prioritised evangelism as primary, or part of, or parallel with their community connections. In the growing churches evangelism was the priority activity, or at least equal in priority to social action. Churches with a lower priority and intentionality in evangelism, such as in Liberal, *Missio Dei* and Emergent churches, did not grow at the same rate, if at all. Evangelism, by adding new people to the local church and its mission, was also seen to be essential to the on-going viability of the mission.

Some leaders and churches were seeking to evangelise those still in existing chapels, as a distinct mission field, but this was a rapidly diminishing target for mission. Others, leading traditional churches, sought to engage in mission through new activities, in existing chapel buildings. These might be new groups such as *Messy Church,* or alternative services, groups and communities. In these approaches, some of the familiar religious patterns of hymnology, buildings, and local connections could be retained, thus avoiding local suspicion. In these ways, evangelism can be sensitive to Welsh religious traditions, loyalties, sentiment and awareness, where their lack would lead to a perceived Englishness. However, most of the population of Wales are either un-churched or de-churched, and so not responsive to church based activities and programmes. Mission to the un-churched has to involve more than church style, symbols or pulpit sermons, if it is to gain a hearing or have a beneficial effect on its community.

Equally, the nature of the message would seem to require right content and a deep conviction and intentionality in those doing the mission. Downplaying the importance of individual salvation, reconciliation with a holy God, forgiveness, new life and hope, neither motivated mission nor

> ### *Sounding* Sense
>
> ....
>
> There was concern expressed in the groups that the gospel was losing its central place, and that there was confusion, even among leaders, as to what the gospel is. *"The foundational gospel seems to be taking a back seat. Having an authentic belief in the fundamentals. Hell seems to have disappeared from the vocabulary of my tradition. There seems to be things put on the back burner and the gospel is not proclaimed with conviction and power"* ... *"The gospel has lost its power. The churches are doing things, but need to get hold of the gospel and really communicate it. We've lost sight of sharing the gospel with our neighbours"* and that there was a *"need to reclaim a confidence in the gospel"*. It was felt that there would be *"fewer churches but better churches... those that are gospel centred, gospel focussed, mixing that with a concern and a compassion for the community. Outward looking, authentic"*.
>
> ....

convinced the hearer. General notions of the love of God, his acceptance and benevolence, did not challenge people about their need or call for a clear response. Encouraging people on a spiritual journey may have no clear point of commitment or experience of forgiveness and acceptance. E2 and Lausanne *Approaches* gave priority to these elements, so their apparent effectiveness cannot be put down merely to the fact that they were very involved in social action.

Social Action as a Component of Mission

Some of a local church's recorded connections to their community were organised, initially, and in some cases primarily, for their own members and attendees. Up to five activities (for children, youth, elderly, counselling and the use of their building) were identified in this category. Therefore, churches that had more than five connections, and in particular those with seven or more connections, demonstrated a greater intentional connectivity with their communities, for the community's benefit. When the proportion of each *Approach* to mission that were found to be growing (5:2 churches: Chart 68) and the proportion that had more than five or seven connections (>5, >7 churches: Chart 69) is compared, a correlation is evident. E2 churches had the most connections to their communities, and had a greater proportion of churches growing 5:2. The charts demonstrate the need for mission that makes the communication of message a priority, and the growth of E2 and Lausanne churches also demonstrates quite conclusively the importance of mission in word and deed, and not just in word or deed only.

E2 and Lausanne churches also have the greater scale and variety of social action programmes. The lower priority given to proclamation in *Missio Dei*, Liberal and Emergent churches did not lead to a higher commitment to community involvement. On the contrary, the churches most involved in *Foodbank*, CAP, night shelters, furniture recycling and programmes in cooperation with local authorities were the E2 and Lausanne churches. The Evangelistic motivation seems to give a greater incentive to provide these services to the community. A possible reason for this is that the priority of proclamation makes the churches outward looking, whereas churches without that priority did not have the same incentive for change and departure from centripetal Christendom models of church and mission. Even Emergent churches, where community connections were the highest priority, could become insular without the priority of proclamation.

The lack of community connection and service in E1 churches arose from a desire not to deflect time and resources from proclamation. However, this lack of engagement resulted in activities intended as outreach, whether preaching or work with children, youth and the elderly, being provided largely for the church's own constituency. If proclamation is equated with preaching within the confines of a church building, it would inevitably be preaching to the already converted. As a result, such proclamation had few new hearers. They lacked the social capital, as well as the relationships, to gain a wider hearing. A secular, post-Christendom and largely post-Christian Wales did not have the loyalty, or sense of obligation, to attend places of worship. According to the 2007 *Tearfund* survey, half the population considered themselves de-churched, unwilling to return. If the churches do not build bridges to their communities, the population appears unlikely to reconsider Christian commitment or an openness to a Christian message. However, as governments cut back on social provision, the opportunities for churches to connect with and affect their communities, present open opportunities for mission:

> "In the Welsh Valleys the churches are being given an opportunity to meet the needs that nobody else is reaching. Our extremity is God's opportunity and a platform to meet the needs that people are crying out for. Certainly the local council see the relevance. In our valley it is the church that is doing the one *Foodbank*."

The future of mission in Wales will need to mix proclamation with provision for community need.

The Miraculous as a Component of Mission

The global growth of Pentecostal and Charismatic churches has been described in Section One. Their approach to mission gives a high priority to the supernatural, and miraculous signs, as a means of validating their message. McClymond describes how this approach is rooted in an attempt to rediscover New Testament approaches and success in mission:

> "The *charismatic* tradition of mission was conspicuous during the church's
> first two centuries and has been revived during the last 150 years in the global
> evangelical missionary movement and among Pentecostal and Charismatic
> Christians. A key idea is that the verbal presentation of the good news should
> be accompanied by tangible signs of God's presence and power".[174]

During the 1980s, Wimber had used the term "power evangelism" to
describe the combination of proclamation evangelism with supernatural
demonstration. This tradition has been maintained and promoted by the
New Wine Cymru (NWC) network, which emphasises the importance
of the miraculous in the life and mission of the local church, as a way
of gaining a hearing for the church's message. The *Waleswide* Survey of
2012 did not have a specific question on this approach to mission, but
some responses to the questionnaire and interviews did reference the
miraculous, at least anecdotally.

This aspect of mission seeks to reconnect with the miraculous elements
in the New Testament in order to see similar evangelistic outcomes.
Pentecostal leaders, many of whom are part of NWC, would also hold
such views, at least in theory, and many would seek to actively practice
them. NWC, in its "Healing Menu", encourages a number of practices
designed to take the miraculous work of the Holy Spirit out of a church
context and into the community:

> "The Healing and Evangelism Menu has been designed with the un-churched
> in mind. The aim is for local churches to provide a variety of opportunities
> for people to receive prayer for healing and discover Jesus in a natural, non-
> threatening and down-to-earth manner".[175]

---

174 McClymond, "Mission and Evangelism," in McDermott, *Evangelical Theology*, 5.
175 "New Wine Cymru Healing: Healing Menu," http://newwinecymru.co.uk/healing-campaign/.

> ### *Sounding* Sense
>
> ....
>
> The expectation that God is seen to be at work in live churches gave a real sense of confidence. People needed to see what real Christianity was like. *"There are opportunities in the community. They are willing to accept the church ... We have been getting back into the whole area of healing, Jesus' gospel, the kingdom of God ... seeing that as a way for engaging with people, for them to see God working in their own lives. There is a developing spirituality outside, but rejecting traditional Christianity".*
>
> ....

The NWC website provides podcast testimonies of healing, some resulting in people finding faith for the first time. The NWC network, of more than 600 Pentecostal and Charismatic church leaders, would certainly call into question Bruce's comment that the Charismatic Movement fades the farther one moves away from the south-east of England.[176] The anecdotal reports of additions to the Christian faith were not on a sufficient scale to show a widespread growth in local churches. However, this approach to mission, with connections into many communities in Wales has developed on a scale to be considered as a serious approach, not only to enhance the Christian message but also as a response to community needs.

Church Planting as a Component of Mission

Liberal churches have maintained the traditional expression of church and mission. Together with *Missio Dei* churches, they have been active in ecumenical initiatives to amalgamate churches and denominations,

---

176 S. Bruce, "Religion in Rural Wales: Four Restudies," *Contemporary Wales* 23 (2010): 232.

in order to stem the rate of decline. Bosch, one of the primary shapers of a *Missio Dei Approach*, wrote against the planting of new churches. He maintained that, with the end of Christendom, church planting would be the Church pointing to itself, as an expression of denominational expansionism. The Church, according to Bosch, needed to point, instead, to God, and what he was doing in the world generally, both now and in the future.[177] However, in the New Testament new churches were an inevitable consequence of evangelistic proclamation. New churches formed the bases from which further mission could take place, which led to societal change, rather than the reverse as Bosch appears to argue.

Emergent churches had attempted to start afresh, but encountered difficulties and suspicion as they sought to develop new, non-traditional, expressions of local church in Wales. The traditional form, and its negative associations in the Welsh *psyche,* may need to pass from society's memory before another form can take its place. However, the possibility has also been suggested that the decline experienced in some *Approaches* is the result of an oblique approach to evangelism. This is supported by the fact that new Evangelistic church plants in English language areas have survived, and even grown. Welsh language communities have not been as receptive to new models, and progress has been with the younger generations. They have less loyalty to family chapels, and are more open to the contemporary and unstructured approach of the new churches. The new plants that have made progress in Welsh language and traditional communities are often re-plants into chapel buildings that were in danger of closing. They retain elements of traditional Welsh chapel, including the Welsh language where it is appropriate. Such renewed congregations are contemporary in approach, and missional in their approach, but retain a deliberate Welshness.

---

177 Bosch, *Transforming,* 332.

Sounding **Sense**

....

The closure of traditional chapels, especially in rural areas, made the need for church planting a high priority. Several references were made to Wales being *"a land of villages"*, so *"Our expectation in Wales is not to see churches of thousands, but thousands of churches. The Welsh demographics and geography would lead us to expect smaller groups in many communities, but linked relationally and sometimes organisationally"*. The need for *"some new beginnings. Green field, brown field. Green field not always possible. Re-planting sometimes better"*. Brown field represented re-planting on an existing chapel site, so building on existing community connections: *"Re-planting is the key element"*. However, *"There will then be a need to plant into the spaces left by the closing chapels. There will be revitalisation, where people are willing, but they won't be many. The day of waiting out of respect for an existing chapel to close before planting is coming to an end. Younger people have no loyalty to denominations at all"*... *"We need new models, sometimes we seem to be trying to reproduce the past. We are trying to reproduce something Victorian. If we go back 100 years before that, Wales had the new church planting models that everyone is talking about"*... *"A new church will come out of the old thing. The church needs to change, let go of its buildings, and be re-born in the parlour"*. *God is clearing the ground to do a new work. Changing patterns of church and ministry ... Groups of people ... Tent-making ministry, not expecting support... Cross-community gatherings, using the web. Community, informal, not chapel. Members doing the ministry, teams, using gifts, delegation ... Change will enable change. ... We have a great hope ... in a great God. Mustn't lose sight that He does new things"*.

....

Church planting has been described by Wagner as "the most effective form of evangelism under heaven",[178] and if there are to be living churches in parts of Wales that have, or will become church-less, there may not

---

178 C. P. Wagner, *Church Planting for Greater Harvest* (Glendale: Regal, 1991), 5.

be another option. Timmis and Chester contend that new church plants encourage higher levels of participation and inclusion than traditional churches:

> "...church planting creates a simplicity that prevents a maintenance mentality - there are no expensive buildings to maintain or complex programmes to run... the priesthood of all believers finds fullest expression when nobody's contribution gets lost in the crowd."[179]

For them, a loving community is the basis of the Church's witness, and its best apologetic, with further church communities planted as the ongoing outcome.[180] For Van Gelder and Zscheile, church planting is a necessary missional activity, which is not burdened by the challenges associated with changing the ingrained patterns of an established church.

Reflections on Adjustments to the Religious Context

If there is to be a Christian presence in most areas of Wales by the middle of the twenty-first century, new churches with a new expression of church and mission will inevitably be necessary. Churches will need to be orientated to holistic mission, as their *raison d'être,* and not see mission as merely an activity for their own survival. They will need to be missional in their orientation, and seen as contemporary, relevant, and part of the community, not remote from it.

Leaders, from contrasting *Approaches* to mission, commented that churches in their area, that will remain in the future, will be contemporary and Pentecostal, in contrast to the traditional Welsh chapel model, which will be extinct:

---

179 S. Timmis and T. Chester, *Gospel-Centred Church* (New Malden: Good Book Company, 2002), 90.
180 T Chester and S. Timmis, *Total Church: A Radical Reshaping Around Gospel and Community* (Leicester: IVP, 2007), 54-55, 64-66, 83-86.

"I've got to be honest, the present generation of the Chapel has not done any favours... the generation that was before me was just a facade. It (the future) will be dominated by Pentecostal churches, English language, and with all the dead chapels dead and closed".

It was felt that these would represent "a much more true picture of authentic Gospel Christianity". Even those who did not share the theological convictions of these churches, or their style of church and mission, recognised the reality:

"I think that some of the churches, probably this one included, I don't see how it will still be here, quite honestly... I just can't see it continuing... There is one church that might still be here... they are not Pentecostal but they are heading that way. ... I can see that that will still be going...".

There was also an awareness that, though the chapel culture is no longer relevant, and a contemporary approach is needed, the religious expression will need to be Welsh in feel, not English. This represents a tension between the old, for which some loyalty remains, and the new, which will be more meaningful to contemporary Wales. It is a challenge that is especially Welsh, and one which will need a different response in particular parts of Wales.

Geographical:
Where We Do Church

The geographical contexts in Wales have been shown to have promoted a profound sense of localism, with a loyalty to a community's *milltir sgwar* or *bro*. *Brogarwch* (love of local) has been seen to be even stronger than *gwladgarwch* (love of nation). Localism has also been identified in urban areas, where adjacent communities are perceived as distinct villages. Such localism has been seen to affect people's experience, perspective, and their leadership:

> "Those born and raised here, I think it's as if they haven't tasted the real world. They have been so isolated. I remember when I first came here I met farmers who would never ever have been out of Wales, and some of them not out of mid Wales".

In the Valleys, this has produced a sense of enclave, a society that is strongly bounded and is suspicious of outsiders.

Therefore, models of mission that are effective in other areas of Britain, or beyond, may not be as suited to Wales, and especially rural areas. Rowan Williams' uneasiness about applying urban programmes to rural contexts will be particularly appropriate in Wales:

> "It will not do in our mission to assume that evangelism and the routine of worship in the countryside can or should be a straight transfer from urban, let alone suburban, patterns; some of the malaise and frustration that are felt in rural churches have to do with this, as well as with expectations that are brought in from elsewhere".[181]

---

181 S. Gaze, *Mission-Shaped and Rural* (London: Church House, 2007), x.

***Sounding* Sense**

Ministry will be part or spare time, and planting will be by teams who live locally, or move to join a plant: *"it can only be local...need to encourage a commitment to the local, not commuting out of the area. Need to reach local people, disciple the people, loving the people"*... *"We need to live on the front line, to reach the specific local needs by involvement in the local community"*.

This statement is doubly pertinent, not only in respect to localism, but also because of how alien approaches from across borders will be received. Where suburban religion does exist in Wales' cities, the patterns of larger churches, with multiple facilities and programmes, will be neither appropriate, possible, nor welcome in smaller communities. The local *cynefin*, the Welsh word for 'habitat' or 'place', will need to be considered carefully, and contextualised mission will need to be adjusted to it. The challenge of declining churches, rural depopulation, and diminishing social cohesion, is an increasing challenge for mission in Wales. The historic patterns of church are increasingly unsustainable, and any urban models of church and mission are difficult to introduce or sustain more widely. The enormity of the challenge of Wales' relatively small communities was evident in the questionnaire and interview responses, in which several approaches were suggested.

A Policy of Centralisation

Firstly, there were ministers who saw no future for churches in small rural communities. Such an assessment could arise from pessimism or pragmatism. Ministers of Liberal churches, who had only ever seen the chapels dwindling and closing, were honestly pessimistic. Likewise, traditional *Missio Dei* leaders hoped for better things, but felt hampered by inflexible structures.

Some churches and leaders were pragmatic and positive about the problems, adopting a different approach. If ministry and mission were unsustainable in small rural or Valley communities, then regional centres should serve a wider area. One church which had tried, largely unsuccessfully, to plant daughter churches in smaller communities, is hoping to build a community resource for the locality, with nursery, gym, café, and conferencing facilities. The vision is to draw people to a regional centre, in the same way that hospitals, supermarkets and schools increasingly draw people from a wider area. Resources would be in the central location, and programmes organised there, rather than in each community. Such a policy does not seek to calibrate to local communities, or *brogarwch*, and would tend to draw only those with an existing desire to be part of Christian community, and willing to travel the distances involved. Such an approach, unless it also had many local expressions, would not be equipped to provide local ministry or mission, apart from the local witness and service of individual commuting Christians. It is difficult to see how mission could serve and transform smaller communities on such a model. People would travel to receive services, be they *Foodbank*, gym, nursery or counselling, but the building of relationships, pastoral care or systematic evangelism and mission would be problematic. It may also be that only people who have moved into the area would be willing to travel, with the indigenous Welsh population seeing commuting as an alien idea. In which case, mission to scattered communities would remain ineffective.

A Policy of Multiplication

Secondly, there were leaders who want mission to be present and effective locally in the smaller towns and villages. Mission, to them, must reflect, be part of, and be incorporated into the local community. Particular contexts may be understandable only from within, so small missional communities, which are embedded in the community, will be more effective than larger churches that gather from many localities.[182] These churches and leaders resource regional branch congregations, or local Christian communities, as part of one church structure.

This pattern of local mission has a long pedigree in rural Wales. The early Nonconformist practice of county-wide churches, made up of small groups scattered in different communities within the area, had one main centre but many local expressions. In the seventeenth century, "County Churches" had local expressions across the counties of Brecon, Ceredigion, Carmarthenshire, Merioneth, Anglesey, and West Glamorgan. The structure of early Calvinistic Methodism, with its *seiadau*, had the same local expression. Such historic patterns may be contextually appropriate once again in twenty-first century Wales. Larger churches, instead of seeking to draw people into their churches from a wide area, could resource small groups in different areas. The benefits of a large centre, with programmes such as youth work, counselling or *Foodbank*, could then be spread widely. The many local gatherings would also have the benefit of being part of the vision, care and leadership of the central body.

Breen speaks of smaller groups that "orbit round larger churches".[183] For one leader, such groups were essential to make the mission of the

---

182 Timmis and Chester, *Gospel-Centred*, 88.
183 M. Breen, *Leading Missional Communities: Rediscovering the Power of Living on Mission Together* (Pawleys Island: 3DM, 2013), 10.

church relevant and accessible to people's lives, and not just a service provided:

> "My vision would be to see in every street in the (area) a place where there was a house of peace. I don't think that for the community we're reaching at the moment, an hour on a Sunday, or an hour and a half in midweek, is enough. It needs for Jesus to be modelled 24/7 ... They need to hear it but we also need to see, and that will only happen when we become a lot more incarnational in our groups."

In other parts of the UK, and beyond, churches operate multi-site congregations, which are expressions of one central church. They may be made up of a cluster of people or of hundreds, as expressions of one church. Modern technology, using DVD recordings or live-streaming, means that the separate congregations can receive the same quality of teaching and vision, and feel a part of a larger whole, even though separated by distance. With the hoped-for distribution of superfast broadband, such technology could be used in scattered rural and Valley communities in Wales to provide teaching and connection centrally, with mission, community engagement, and pastoral care expressed locally.

Sounding Sense

There was a strong sense of the need for the stronger churches in the cities and larger towns to accept a role as resource churches, under whose care smaller churches might thrive. This involves individual churches reaching out to neighbouring areas, as well as being involved into remoter areas of great need. *"I am expecting great churches in the suburbs of our cities, but unless those churches recognise their responsibility, then Christianity is going to become the privilege of the middle class. There are a lot of people from the Valleys going down to those sort of churches ... dormer towns where people travel to work in the cities ... If the leaders of these churches recognised that we've got people coming from all over ... let's get people together, raise up some leadership within that area and help them to do something where they're at. They could be really serving a kingdom mind-set. Big churches need to take big risks and be willing to lose people"...* "*Growth by people moving in, but also moving into an adjacent area where there is no Bible church as a small group. There is something there of a church taking ownership or responsibility for another area, thinking beyond"...* "*Larger churches are missing a God-given mandate to Judea ... There are great opportunities but few workers. We need a church to come alongside ... there would be two-way benefits"*. There was a sense that the Church as a whole needs to take responsibility for needy areas. Even smaller churches in rural areas could play their part: "*We need to think as missionaries, whether large churches or small... ... churches in the abyss where we are, see ourselves as resourcing churches ... we may be a small church, but we can be a point of influence into the communities near us"*. The model suggested for this, repeated in many *Soundings*, was for "*large churches with local groups"*, either by people moving home, or being involved by travelling to remoter areas. "*There is something there of a church taking ownership or responsibility for another area, thinking beyond"*. For some this involved establishing "*hubs"*, for where "*people are very tribal about where they live ... hubs that are community specific, but also link that community to a much bigger meeting place and organisation"*. Otherwise, "*rural areas will have people travelling from large areas, so more of an emphasis on gospel communities, with a connection to a central leadership. Small clusters with a regional gathering. People travel to successful churches because of a consumer culture. The larger stronger churches need to get alongside to regenerate or take them in. A greater sharing of resources and people resources"*. There can be fewer more important issues for rural areas. Without it, we will continue to see areas and churches "*suffering from 50 years of careful neglect"*... "*the remaining Christians will be more likely to commute further to get to the churches that do exist, and in commuting further they don't necessarily have roots in the community where the church actually exists. There could be a missional community model where the Sunday isn't the only thing. In the week, where the believers are, they are making disciples. Churches become resource centres. There is very little cost with small communities"*.

A Policy of Multiplying of Independent Cells

A third alternative, is the multiplying of independent cell or house churches, sometimes in the form of small church plants. The former would meet in homes, whereas the latter would meet weekly in a public venue, in a form more akin to traditional church patterns. Various approaches to cell and house churches have been popularised in Britain, and internationally, in the late twentieth and twenty-first century. These movements represent a significant shift away from traditional congregational structures:

> "... these groups were to become *the actual primary experience of church* rather than just being a program of the church. Each of these groups is a church in its own right. This is a big shift."[184]

The cells are mostly independent, being a church in and of themselves, or in a loose relational network with other cell or house churches. There was, however, little or no evidence, as with the small Emergent churches, that such cells multiplied successfully in Wales in the first decade of the twenty-first century.

Starting and Resourcing Local Churches

Section Two showed the need for a new and relevant expression of church that would be effective locally. The need for a fresh start was seen as compelling and urgent:

> "There will be different shapes, the same principles in the same truths, but I can see in some of the smaller villages a house group, small groups, and a presence in certain places looking very different to what the church would look like in the middle of (town). I see a more fluid approach, retaining all the doctrine, but tailored to where they are situated."

---

184 Hirsch, *Forgotten*, 46.

The establishing of small cells or churches in areas where churches have closed or are closing, could be attempted by gathering the remnants of churches that are closing; by Christians who had been commuting to church outside their area forming church in their locality; or by larger churches relocating members into a needy area. This might be the result of individual, church or denominational strategic planning, or the concerned response of a few, "a *bubble up* strategy, which means average Christians get a burden to begin a new church".

Sounding Sense

In thirteen of the Soundings, there was a strong sense that relational cooperation was the only way to address Wales' needs. "*When we work together we are stronger. When churches with a like-mindedness, with passion, there is a strength that comes from relationships together in God-honouring churches. Others come on board and are encouraged by the momentum that that brings. There is something special about networks ... a terrific strength*"... "*It is not just a fraternity. There is meaningful relationship, shared experience, genuine love, and relationship ... partnership for the gospel*". Denominations were seen to be working together more, with a breaking down of denominational barriers. "*It is much more about relationships, friendships and partnerships through choice. We mission out of our relationships*".

Some leaders and churches hold the conviction that "churches plant churches", whereas others hope to see church communities develop more organically. For others, the renewal of existing chapel communities, or re-planting in a closing building, would be more appropriate. Such an approach would give an ongoing link within the locality and its history, and so be more easily accepted in traditional communities. Whatever the approach, however, these attempts to renew or re-establish Christian communities in local areas will be seeking to do mission from within the community, rather than from without.

The support, training, and oversight of such smaller congregations, and their leaders, is a vital factor in their survival and growth. Where local Christian communities are expressions or one larger regional church, support and training would be provided by the parent church. Other church plants would look to the denomination, network or church which planted them. Churches or cells formed by individuals, without wider connections or accountability, have been very vulnerable in times of loss, trial or internal conflict. Some churches are overseen by teams which have a relational, and often informal connection with local leaders and churches, as distinct from traditional denominational allegiances.

Reflections on Adjustments to the Geographical Contexts

The presence of a strong sense of localism in all areas of Wales, suggests that mission, as well as church, needs to be local. Establishing large church centres, that draw Christians out of their local communities for worship, will mean that in order to benefit from mission would also require travel. For that reason, such an approach would seem to be against the grain of Welsh geographical contexts. A leader of a church adopting such a policy expressed frustration with leaders and members who came from the local area, saying that people from England were more proactive and enthusiastic. This may reflect ethnic factors, which will be considered in the following section, but it may also demonstrate a reluctance in people with strong local loyalties, to travel, and to be part of such a model.

Wales, being a land of villages, will need local mission. Initiatives to renew, replant, gather, or relocate Christians in a specific local community seem to be the only way for mission to be indigenous and geared to that locality. There are few other options available for rural areas, or for smaller communities within a locality or strata of urban society. If separate communities in Wales are to benefit from Christian mission, that mission will need to be local, and calibrated to the particular needs and characteristics of that locality.

Ethnic:
Who Are We Reaching?

A diversity of ethnic identity has been identified among people living in Wales, and in the different regions of Wales. The contrasting identities make up a shared national awareness, but they are markedly different, even conflicting, in their understanding of Welshness. Those who see themselves as a part of a British set, would be regarded as a threat in communities valuing an inherited genetic Welshness, and the subject of derision in Valley areas. Effective mission will need to calibrate differently to such contrasting identities.

Sounding Sense

"The thousands of Syrians are going to end up in the Valleys. We must be ready... we will be the ones welcoming them. We need to start training... there have been repeated waves of immigration into the Valleys. Our communities are changing, so we need to start thinking how we help that. The ethnic minorities are becoming the ethnic substantial".

In urban, cosmopolitan communities, minority ethnic communities also require a sensitive approach to mission for their particular *ethnie*. However, whether mission calibrated for a specific *ethnie* should be the responsibility of a separate church, made up of that *ethnie,* is a matter of debate. In Cardiff, mono-ethnic churches have been formed for people from Arabic, Chinese, Korean, Persian and West African backgrounds. However, other churches would encourage integration, not separate development, and see the multi-national nature of the local church as one of their strengths and achievements in the midst of racial tension and suspicion.

These different responses to the various ethnic identities in Wales reveal the challenges that ethnic factors present to mission. A desire for multi-ethnicity to be modelled in the local church is in contrast to those who recognise separate communities, and call for mono-ethnic churches and mission.

A Policy of Distinction

Some churches, notably those for immigrant communities in cities, or Welsh language churches in *y Fro Gymraeg*, were mono-ethnic in their ministry and mission. They were adopting, whether intentionally or not, Donald A. McGavran's "Homogeneous Unit Principle" which maintained that people come to faith most easily through their own culture and language, without crossing racial, linguistic, class or cultural barriers. Churches, therefore, need to be planted for single cultures and language groups, and not as multi-racial and multi-lingual communities. He argued that unbelievers understand the gospel better when expounded by their own kind of people.[185]

Some Welsh communities form a distinct or parallel community to people who have moved from England into their area, and some Welsh churches have located themselves within their ethnic group, to reach and serve that group exclusively. They maintain that ethnic distinctions were God-given and should be preserved.[186] Kreitzer contended that single ethnic churches were particularly important when considering church

---

185 D. A. McGavran, *Understanding Church Growth* (Grand Rapids: Eerdmans, 1976), 167, 198-215.
186 Jones, *Faith*, 86-88, 94, 206-207; Jones, *Crist a Chenedlaetholdeb*, 9-10, 30, 37, 46.

planting,[187] an issue of critical importance in *y Fro Gymraeg*. For a new church to make an effective initial connection with a community was critical for its survival.

A Policy of Integration

Another approach to the issue, however, calls for integration, not separation. Malcom regarded Christian communities as *"in principle* always multicultural communities" (italics his).[188] Breaking down ethnic barriers is to be an essential aspect of the gospel, and to defend mono-ethnic churches would be denying catholicity in a Church that is "irreducibly multicultural". Malcolm sees integration as an inevitable consequence of the Spirit's work, whilst, at the same time including an acceptance of difference and particularity, a unity in diversity. Such inclusivity is seen as all the more important in a post-modern age, where pluralism and difference are no longer threatening:

> "While other institutions are desegregating, with diversified schools and workplaces, multicultural congregations will make more sense to the next generation than monocultural ones do".[189]

For others, mono-ethnic congregations were little more than a cultural comfort zone, despite what may be perceived as a greater cultural authenticity leading to some evidence of growth. Ultimately, it makes no more sense in biblical terms to have a 'black church' or a 'white church' than it does to have a 'rich church' or a 'poor church'. Instead, a

---

187 M. R. Kreitzer, *Good News for All People: Towards a Biblical Theology of Ethnicity and Mission* (Birmingham: Birmingham Theological Seminary, 2004), 5, 297.

188 L. Malcolm, "Raised for Our Justification: Christ's Spirit for Us and for All," in *Created and Led by the Spirit: Planting Missional Congregations* (ed. M. Dreier; Grand Rapids: Eerdmans, 2013), 64-66.

189 Malcolm, "Raised for Our Justification," in Dreier, *Missional Congregations*, 173-174.

multi-ethnic church would benefit from the challenge of other cultures. Alternatively, mono-ethnic churches might exist for a limited period, while people adjust to alien cultural practices, but only as "a 'half-way house', with the ultimate target being to meet as part of a united, multi-ethnic fellowship".

For those seeking multi-ethnic churches and mission, a mono-ethnic approach was akin to apartheid. It was potentially "bad news", causing Christians to "live a self-centred, impoverished life", if it was not overthrowing racial, cultural and class barriers. It could only be justified, in the short term, if it would lead to a multi-ethnic and multi-racial church.

These arguments, however, have to assume that mono-ethnic churches in Wales are not working as partners, and cooperating with churches of a different *ethnie* wherever possible. This, in fact, has been far from the case, with churches connecting, and even planting, across ethnic lines. The Evangelical Church in Bangor was a bilingual church, with language groups meeting separately and together, that decided to become two mono-ethnic churches. In a similar way, a number of English language churches in south Wales were started by Welsh language churches to serve the English-speaking immigrants at the time of industrial expansion. Churches serving different ethnic communities, working together on projects such as *Foodbank*, CAP, or night-shelter, send messages of unity and cohesion, rather than the contrary. Such mission expresses unity between churches and Christians, whilst at the same time respecting differences in ethnic identity. For McGavran, working within a distinct ethnicity was a bridge that enabled mission to take place, in and by people of that *ethnie*. In areas of Wales, such as *y Fro Gymraeg*, to work multi-ethnically would generate resistance and limit a mission's effectiveness. In fact, cooperative mission by churches serving Welsh and English communities could model a community cohesion that minimises suspicion and enmity. Forcing communities together, or insisting that one has to conform to the patterns or language of another, would tend to exacerbate negative positions.

If the Church in a town or region is seen to be one in its mission, but focussing on different spheres, the charge of acting contrary to the gospel, or neglecting its essential elements, is difficult to sustain.

The Implications for leadership

The ability, and acceptability, of leadership is essential to any mission. In areas of Wales where there is a strong Welsh identity, whether in the post-industrial Valleys or *y Fro Gymraeg*, those doing or leading mission will be seen as an insider or an outsider, depending on their own background:

> "It takes a bit of time for people from outside to be trusted, especially with the gospel message. They would want to know who is he related to, does he have any links to (place)..."

Suspicion and even resistance can be generated by those doing the mission. Equally, in areas with a heterogeneous population, whether in urban or in a border community, working to the exclusion of some in the community would appear equally alien. The context has an important bearing on how mission is done and led, and how leaders are trained.

In the traditional model of leadership and mission in Wales, from the mid-nineteenth century, ministry and mission were led by ordained ministers. They would have received a formal training in theology, but may not have had their roots in the community they served. Their status as a minister, and their superior educational qualifications, gave them acceptance in the communities they moved to in the course of their professional career.

Not only has the decline of Nonconformity made such a model of ministry unsustainable financially, but such a model of ministry or mission is no longer meaningful, except in traditional communities where old patterns still linger. In post-Christian Wales, those leading and doing mission will need to gain acceptance and credibility in the communities they serve. In the Valleys, mission conducted by local people, and led by leaders from those communities, avoids the stigma of Englishness, or resistance to historic patterns of minister-centred mission. In *y Fro Gymraeg* local leaders avoid the resistance to fears of domination by incomers from England. Mission, however well intended, that is conducted in a way that is perceived as being English, or "pushy", "arrogant" or "a take-over", will be resisted. Where a church's mission is being organised, planned and delivered by non-Welsh people, great care will be needed to respect local sensitivities. A church planted in a Welsh area, by a church close to the English border, closed because of these issues:

> "...for them their lives were interconnected, wired in with Chapel, that they were never going to become part of a new church in (place). And of course the people who pioneered the meeting were English people as well...".

The leader of the planting church put the issue starkly:

> "There is some Welshness where people are strongly defensive... It's almost as if somehow, like the invasions of the past, when you come to them with something that is like the gospel, they feel threatened and close in, and that gets deeper the farther west you go from here."

Methods of mission originating in England and, in this case, another part of Wales, were seen as threatening. Both leaders and methods, which were from outside of Wales, encountered a similar resistance.

Outside major towns and cities, leadership of ministry and mission will increasingly be done by lay leaders, or part-time leaders. The absence of individuals who are paid full-time, so having time to do activities on behalf of the members, will have to be replaced by teams of local people. The benefits of such a change, in terms of mission being done on a peer level by neighbours, is self-evident. Clericalism did not engender a corporate ownership of the mission of the church.

The training of leaders and churches for mission will need to be contextualised to the local situation, and be provided locally. Part-time or lay leaders will not have the liberty, time, or the resources, to go away to a place of training.

In the questionnaire and interview response of leaders, repeated reference was made to a reticence, shyness, and lack of confidence, commitment and perseverance among Welsh people, compared to those who had moved into the church and wider community from England. One leader described the issue bluntly:

> "...small-mindedness, defensiveness, lack of ambition, very easily satisfied with what they've got ...to be honest I can't see how we could ever have a leadership team of just Welsh people. Any life in our church, any strong ambition to win people, to get out there, comes from the English".

Another spoke of a lack of ambition, and a lack of urgency to change things:

> "I think Wales has a 'that will do' attitude ... what they have they always want, rather than expressions of something greater. ... We don't look for anything grander, anything better. Because people are stuck with change... My hardest people to motivate are the Welsh-speaking, it seems."

The same phenomenon was described in the Valleys, where generations of decline and a "siege mentality" had produced a generation which felt they had nothing to offer, despite being no less gifted: "...I think you can't underestimate what happened with the close of the pits... We're rubbish. There is absolutely no aspiration at all." One leader expressed the reality in typical humour: "Murphy's Law says that if anything can go wrong it will. Jones's law says that Murphy was an optimist." The lack of confidence has also been seen as a reason to invite people into leadership, and not merely to ask for volunteers:

> "It's quite odd really, very low self-worth. You very rarely get someone to volunteer for something, but if you ask someone, wow! ... It is as if they grow 10 feet tall - he thinks I am good enough to be asked. They have such low self-worth, so if you ask someone you are dealing with a different person. It's incredible the difference it can make".

Clearly, training of leaders that affirms and builds a confidence to lead is important, alongside theoretical and applied theology. Training programmes, or approaches to mission, that work in other nations may fail to develop missional leaders in Wales. A greater level of affirmation, encouragement and team support will be needed if there is a sense of inertia, hopelessness, or lack of entrepreneurial drive. This may be attributed to different causes, whether years of church decline or a consequence of colonisation, but Dr Dilys Davies's call for extra provision in public health may have its equivalent in mission training.

Sounding Sense

In each *Sounding* a concern for adequate and relevant training was expressed. Training one theological leader was no longer seen as adequate. Churches needed to be led by teams, where all members received training in discipleship, theology and ministry. All members needed to be equipped and active, not a clerical few. Without a multiplying of younger leaders, no new mission to Wales will be possible. Most saw this training as best provided locally, by groups or networks of churches, in a way that is *"training gospel community leaders... a change of culture ... organic and vocational"*. A need was expressed for *"gap year"* training in rural Wales, *"identifying calling, training in vocation, apprenticing, informing, and stretching theologically"*. *"Surely, the local church should be the place where they are equipped, where they are trained, where they grow, where they are living it and doing it as well as being trained. The nature of theological training must change ... Training leaders and every role. Each church needs to be a lay seminary where we are training people for ministry in the local environment. ... Training involves a strategy. Training for mission. If there is unity among the churches there is an opportunity to share resources amongst the churches in training"* ... *"Investment in people ... we've got to invest in the future"*.

Reflections on Adjustments to the Ethnic Context

The differing identities of British, Welsh, Welsh-British, or having descended from Celtic ancestors have been seen to call for varying approaches, not only to the nature of mission, but also who does it, and how it is done. Wales is a nation of contrasting and even conflicting ethnic groups, and where the distinctions in adjacent communities are marked, they may be better served by a homogeneous approach in mono-ethnic communities than by a heterogeneous approach in multi-ethnic communities. This would better serve the mission of the church, as long as unity between churches and leaders was expressed.

Though the Lausanne Movement favoured multi-ethnic over mono-ethnic churches, they did recognise the importance of churches contextualising for their mission:

"... the barriers to the acceptance of the gospel are often more sociological than theological; people reject the gospel not because they think it is false but because it strikes them as alien. They imagine that in order to become Christians they must renounce their own culture, lose their own identity, and betray their own people. Therefore, in order to reach them, not only should the evangelist be able to identify with them, and they with the evangelist; not only must the gospel be contextualized in such a way that it communicates with them; but the church into which they are invited must itself belong to their culture sufficiently for them to feel at home in it".[190]

---

190 J. R. W. Stott, ed., *Explaining the Gospel in Today's World: Church Planting - The Homogeneous Unit* (London: Scripture Union, 1978), *Unit*, 5.

Language and Culture: Welsh, English or Both?

The Welsh language has created and sustained its own distinct culture. Its decline has been described: from a time when Wales was a land of monoglot Welsh speakers; to three language corridors running from north to south, with Welsh speakers only dominant in the West; to the present patchwork with small remnant areas of majority-Welsh speakers. At the same time Welsh medium education is seeing a rapid rise in all parts of Wales, so the Welsh language demographic, which was dominated by the older generations, is now showing signs of a burgeoning younger profile. This Welsh language renaissance, if the younger generations continue to use the language, will have a profound effect on the changing mission context. Currently, the language is both a marker of unity and of division, with insistence on its place in society in some areas and resistance in others. Expressions of culture largely follow this divide. Mission will need to calibrate to such realities.

The case for and against mono-ethnic churches has been considered. Issues of language and culture are an aspect of ethnicity, and the various adjustments to language and culture in mission mirror the same polarities. In Welsh language areas, the appropriateness of Welsh language churches is a major issue for mission. In urban, Valleys and border areas, it is the challenge of identifying the Anglo-Welsh culture, and calibrating mission to that.

Welsh Language Churches

Welsh language churches grew up, or have been more recently planted, in Welsh language communities. These may be rural communities or a stratum of society in towns or cities. They seek to work entirely through the medium of Welsh in their ministry and mission. Welsh is not merely used in mission, but is the preferred medium for worship and relationships, for people who think, live and pray through the medium of Welsh:

> "The most important and the most intimate thing in someone's life is their relationship with Jesus. Therefore, it is natural for a Welsh speaker to want that relationship to be in their heart language".

Some churches provide simultaneous translation for visitors, or for English-speaking partners, or the family of members. Some also hold occasional English or bilingual services, or look for an English congregation to provide for English-speakers. Services and courses for Welsh learners are also held, which are intended as a gateway into the main church activities, but held separately from them.

Mission in Welsh language churches might also be done, for the benefit of English speakers, as in the case of *Foodbank*, CAP or *Street Pastors*, but the primary focus of mission, and especially evangelism, is to the Welsh-speaking community. These churches see English language mission in Welsh language areas as introducing an unhelpful hurdle to a reception of the mission and the message:

> "...if the gospel came to them in English they would see it as a foreign idea. If the gospel is presented to them in Welsh it is much more likely for them to listen because it came to them through a medium that they are open to".

Where children's and youth work is done in English in Welsh communities:

"The effect of this is that local Welsh people, who do not know Jesus, see the Christian faith as an anglicising medium and an attack on Welsh... They must earn the right to speak about Jesus in Welsh communities, and the way to do this is through learning the language. The language is important, but the success of the gospel is more important".

The leader was not saying that he would prefer no mission, rather than mission in English, but that if mission was to be effective, it had to be in Welsh, the heart language of the people.

As with reactions to mono-ethnic churches, the existence of Welsh language churches provokes an equal and opposite response. Mention has been made of the comments by the International Director of the Lausanne Movement in favour of multi-ethnic and multi-linguistic churches. He conceded that there might be a case for single-language churches, but as an exception, presumably where it was the only language in a community. He contended that the New Testament Church was transcultural and cut across language divides:

"...when people see there are churches that reach out across ethnic divides, it has a compulsive attractiveness which was there radically in the New Testament. If we emphasise mono-ethnic or mono-cultural churches, sometimes they have to exist for linguistic reasons of course, but if we emphasise that at the expense of the Church of Christ transcending ethnic divisions then our gospel witness will be tempered and weakened".

The elders of an English medium church, that was doing mission in a Welsh language area, put the case even more strongly in a policy document drawn up for their discussions:

"...the planting of separate English speaking and Welsh speaking churches in Wales is contrary to God's stated will in the New Testament, and that the uniting of Welsh speakers and English speakers in local churches is a significant aspect of our witness to the power of the gospel to transform and unite people under the headship of Christ".

The paper conceded that in Welsh language areas there would be more Welsh speakers in a church, but the solution was to be based on the ability to communicate, not for cultural or historical reasons. For the English minority to be able to understand and communicate, this would suggest the use of English as a common medium.

"Central to the demonstration of the power of God in the gospel is that this very diverse company of people are joined together into loving local churches: local churches that, in the language of the creed, are 'catholic': i.e. open to all believers".

The issue of what language was to be used in evangelism was to be determined by the language of the hearers, but once people had joined the church, they would speak the common language. The policy document then stated the overriding principle: "all decisions in the life of the local church must be driven by the gospel". It is this question that the polarised views on Welsh language churches hinges on. If mission is hindered by English being the medium used, whether within the church, or in the wider community, then that mission becomes ineffective, or even nullified. If the very nature of the Church is to be "missional", then that would seem to decide whether mono-lingual churches were not merely permissible, but essential. The fears that mono-lingual churches would be self-centred, impoverished, or a denial of the gospel, are difficult to sustain if using a common language actually hinders mission. The effect and legacy of a dominant English language and culture on its neighbour appears to make common-language churches an actual hindrance, not an advert for the gospel. Phil Hill came to the same conclusion:

"...many Welsh people found (and find) it too difficult to function comfortably in English... This pattern may appear to English people living in monoglot areas to be a contradiction of *the* unity of the Church. But to Welsh people it was the answer of common sense..."[191]

Bilingualism

Bilingualism was a policy adopted by the Anglican Church in Wales, as a response to two language communities in its parishes. Anglicanism had been viewed as an alien, English body, with English-speaking clergy in Welsh-speaking parishes, and suffered as a result in the heyday of Welsh Nonconformity. It later sought to respond better to context by a policy of bilingualism, in which both languages were used equally in its liturgy. A similar policy has been adopted by many churches, especially those in bilingual communities.

"On Sunday morning we have a bilingual service, and that's exactly what it is. Obviously the sermon is in English, and we also have Bible study and prayer meeting which is bilingual... Parents with their children in Welsh school, it suits them to come to a bilingual service... We have taken on board the fact that we have to use both languages."

Two churches, one Welsh and one English, had shared activities, and explained their policy: "We have actively sought not only to use both languages but to encourage an attitude where both languages are not simply 'allowed' but positively affirmed". In a magazine interview, about how to reach families in a bilingual context where half a family speak Welsh and half the family don't, a leader commented:

---

191 P. Hill, "Beyond the Celtic Fringe: Christians and Nationalism in Wales," *Third Way* (April 1978): 8.

"If we want to reach such families we must stop thinking in terms of ministry and mission being either in Welsh or English. To me the key is an incarnational understanding of the Gospel and mission. Where we serve a bilingual community it seems to me that this must be done bilingually".

The practice involves more than mere tokenism, as prayers, songs, literature, publicity and websites, if not preaching, use both languages. In bilingual communities the policy is appreciated because it acknowledges the preferences and traditions of a Welsh-speaking minority, it is helpful for those learning Welsh, and it enables families where only one partner speaks Welsh, or where the children are in Welsh medium education, to worship together. It enabled everyone to worship, and "people of both tongues can encounter God in their heart language".

Classes and services for Welsh learners form an essential part of a bilingual approach:

"...in recognition of the very large number of people locally who are Welsh Learners, we have begun a weekly Conversation Group for Welsh Learners ... Each term we end with a 'Service for Welsh Learners' which is overtly evangelistic in its nature."

Most bilingual churches were English-speaking churches incorporating Welsh, but some Welsh churches were including English in their services, though less successfully:

"Because of the bilingual nature of the community we have provided simultaneous translation in our services. We usually do bilingual services, but they are not often very successful. Therefore, the simultaneous translation means that those who are learning, or pairs where only one can speak Welsh, can come".

Other churches express bilingualism through Welsh language groups formed within an English church, on midweek or Sunday evenings. This might be viewed as a temporary arrangement, until the Welsh group is strong enough to exist as a separate church. However, in other churches there is no intention to separate. In this more common approach, the large number of Welsh speakers, who choose to worship in English medium churches, is a source of tension. The Welsh speakers wish to live and worship in Welsh, but have not found a Welsh church with the right style, theology, resources or family provision. It is also a source of disappointment for those remaining, and struggling, in smaller, and less well-resourced Welsh churches.

In Welsh language areas, bilingualism is viewed as a compromise, threatening the place of Welsh in society. Bilingual conversations, activities and public speaking inevitably revert to English as the common denominator. The English language gains ascendancy, as when a leader said, "I'll say this in English because it's important". This acknowledged that some English speakers might miss the point in Welsh, but failed to recognise that some Welsh speakers often lack confidence in speaking and understanding English. Nevertheless, a bilingual policy, in Welsh language areas, would be considered preferable to the churches that used English as the church's only language. An all-English policy, in a community where most people live through the medium of Welsh, would seem to be impeding mission and making it more difficult for people to hear their message. One English church described the challenge and the frustrations experienced in a Welsh area:

"There is a greater resistance among the Welsh population than among the incomers. As a church we know more incomers. The local people have their networks... The incomers are more open to being befriended, and the indigenous population are suspicious... The sad thing is that the believers are separated by language... they could come, and if we were able to pull in those Welsh speakers who are real believers, and reach Welsh people..." (a greater impact could be achieved).

From this English church leader's perspective, the non-involvement of Welsh speakers in their church blunted their ability to reach the Welsh community. It is, however, questionable, in the light of the comments above, whether such mission from an English-language base would be successful, even if Welsh speakers could be persuaded to join them.

In predominantly English-speaking towns, cities, Valleys and border regions, however, bilingualism is seen as an unwelcome imposition, a waste of time, paper, and resources, in the same way that Welsh Government bilingual forms, signs and publicity are not appreciated by all. However, even in border areas, churches chose to reach out to the minority Welsh speakers, and even made this a distinctive of the church's mission.

"In virtually all parts of Wales there is a Welsh speaking community of some size and churches need to make an effort to reach them – we have had Welsh medium outreach events. If there were sufficient people in the church who were Welsh speaking, we would run a Welsh medium home group ... Other churches have had bilingual singing (projecting the words in English and Welsh)".

If the demographic of Welsh speakers changes, due to Welsh-medium education in all areas, such an approach will become essential and inevitable.

Sounding Sense

There was a general recognition that Welsh language churches were needed to reach Welsh-speaking communities, but that the form of such churches

---

needed to change radically. *"We need to follow the Lord and break the link with Capelyddiaeth... Need to fill the gaps. Increase mutual support and ministry ... to be less tied to church patterns".* Otherwise, Welsh speakers would be travelling farther to church, and often to English language churches, with English & American influences increasing. The opportunities are everywhere, *"On a map of Wales, I could put six pins in where something good is happening. The chapels are at such a point that they have looked into the abyss ... they knew there was no future, so they were willing to do absolutely anything. It cut through all that tradition, and all is up for grabs now".*

Welsh Cultural Mission

Adjustments to Welsh culture, both traditional and popular, for the sake of mission, were generally less evident and deliberate than adjustments to language. Only the Liberal *Approach* saw the promotion of Welsh culture as a central part of its mission, through their high involvement in the cultural activities of the Learning category of mission. They served their communities, particularly the Welsh language communities, by being a focal point for Welsh literary, poetic, historical and community interests. There is little evidence that this led to the growth of the churches, as the churches in question were mostly declining. They did, however, provide a service, together with the involvement of their members in other community activities, for the good of their communities. These activities were provided, for the most part, to the older sections of the community. In reaching younger generations in Welsh communities a different culture was needed:

"I have noticed that the younger generation, they have no Chapel background, and basically even though we speak Welsh they are heavily infected, affected, by English culture... The *Cymanfa Ganu* will bring in the old, and American burger night will bring in the young..."

Clearly, the nature of Welsh culture is changing, at least in part, with the generations.

Other churches made connections with both traditional and popular Welsh culture, as a bridge between the church and its community, especially for evangelism. These activities, described earlier, included events for St David's Day, rugby games, and choral or hymn singing. Evangelism was felt to be more effective when it was "distinctly 'Welsh' in ethos." Some of these activities in English-speaking areas reflect the ongoing cultural influence of the Welsh language, even though the language itself may have faded away. A leader in an English-speaking area of rural mid Wales spoke of their *Cymanfa Ganu*, but singing from "Sankeys", and of an English language *Eisteddfod*. There was a recognition that in both language areas, a Welsh culture was still influential, even when the language had been lost:

> "The ethos of a Welsh church is different. They are not English. They may speak English but they are still Welsh. It must be something to do with tradition, culture and background. A lot of people even though they don't speak Welsh, and wish they could speak Welsh, their mother and father didn't pass it down..."

Reflections on Adjustments to Linguistic and Cultural Contexts

Welsh linguistic and cultural distinctives appeared in a spectrum from communities where the language, and its derived culture, were strong and defended; to those where the language had been largely lost but the cultural traditions remained; to anglicised areas where only traces of Welsh language influence remained. Interspersed within these are micro-communities of Welshness and Englishness that live somewhat detached from the surrounding population.

Where churches were located within a particular micro-community, their mission to the wider community would be impeded.

The controversy over the legitimacy of Welsh language churches showed those for and against, justifying their perspective from biblical precedent. Those opposed to single language churches emphasised the multi-ethnic nature of the church, actively reconciling differences between God and people, and between people. Churches, however, may be involved in a mission against racism, hostility and community tension, without joining in a conglomerate that belongs naturally to neither community.

If linguistic and cultural trends in Wales continue in the direction of bilingualism and Anglicisation, then mission, even in the areas retaining some strength in the Welsh language, will need to follow those trends. If a resurgent Welsh language in schools, media and government leads to a reversal in societal trends, then mission will need to calibrate to that. At the start of the twenty-first century a mixture of English language churches reflecting a popular Welsh culture, English language churches for a traditional culture, bilingual churches, and Welsh language churches will be needed for effective mission.

Social:
Who Are We Serving?

In describing Welsh contexts, a common distinctive of communalism and mutuality was observed. Traditions of an egalitarian society had found expression in the idea of the Nonconformist *Gwerin*, and then in Labourism, as political loyalties replaced chapel allegiance. To varying degrees, and with different expressions, Wales' small local communities still evidence many close-knit, mutually supportive social networks, interconnected by extended families. They are a feature of Wales's social landscape, and mission must adjust to their varying patterns.

The degree of a church's involvement in its community, through relationships, social care and service, will determine whether it is part of its community, or stands apart from it. A local community, in which mutual support and solidarity is the norm, will feel remote from a church that is not an active contributor to that community. To have an attractional, or centripetal, approach to mission, which appears to pull people out of the surrounding society into the church's separate community, will tend to alienate non-attenders. A missional, or centrifugal approach, will bring the church to where people are, and make its religious activities more accessible. Contributing to a community's life and needs are key factors in whether or not a local church is adjusting to its social context, and this will affect how its message is received.

Section Two described how the different *Approaches* to mission had engaged with the social context of Wales, and lessons from each *Approach* were also suggested. These lessons are central to a contextualised mission in Wales, and need to be a significant part of the Church's future strategy.

Rather than repeating the lessons in this chapter, they will be referred to, and the underlying issues will be considered.

The Importance of Social Capital

The work of a local church, meeting the felt needs of its community, is to be part of the "social capital" of that community, and to contribute to it. This will give credibility and receptivity to the church's message.[192] The good news needs to be seen as well as heard:

> "If the purpose of the church is to proclaim and demonstrate the reconciling love of God then the nature of the church is to create the kind of community in which outrageous grace is lived out. People ought to be able to see the values of grace acted out in the kind of community that is created by the gospel".[193]

Gethin Russell-Jones outlines ten activities currently undertaken by local churches, often in partnership with local authorities, which are "changing the face of Wales".[194] They include work with asylum seekers, *Foodbank, Street Pastors,* homes for the homeless, CAP, night shelters, parenting courses, work with refugees, provisions for Welsh-speaking families, and action on human trafficking.

The struggles of many E1 churches, despite much earnest effort and praying, would suggest that the needed connections with their communities, and confidence about them in their communities, were lacking. The changes that have occurred in a post-Christendom era, mean that the once-proven approaches of mission by proclamation and

---

192 Morgan, *Span*, 278.

193 M. Robinson, *Planting Mission Shaped Churches Today* (Oxford: Monarch, 2006), 94.

194 G. Russell-Jones, *Power of 10* (Cardiff: Gweini, 2013), 7-41.

invitation alone, no longer have traction. Helping to build social capital demonstrates a level of relevance and connection that builds confidence and relationships. Without this, the message of the church does not appear to connect with the felt needs of the community it is seeking to reach.

Sounding Sense

In most *Soundings* there was enthusiasm for compassion ministries and how they were the key link with their communities, in which "*The churches are taking ownership of a community vacuum*". We need to be "*a gospel preaching church with a glass of water*". They also said how much churches were cooperating together in Foodbank, youth, CAP, *Street Pastors* ... and that there was a new unity among leaders, and they were talking! It was felt that Local Authorities were engaged with overtly Christian organisations ... "*Foodbank has made the difference in the perception of the church. Not necessarily just in the community itself, but also in the Local Authorities. Foodbank is not overtly evangelistic, but it has certainly provided the platform for further development*".

The Importance of Social Involvement

The legacy of Pietism was that Christians were taken "out of this world", in contrast to a call for the Church to be "incarnational", whereby it is directly engaged with the world's suffering and need. If it stands apart, the Church's mission must be to draw people into its own world by attraction. If it is "incarnational", it is entering the sphere of need in an act of compassion and rescue. The word is used uniquely in how Jesus came, and its use for the Church's mission may seem incongruous, but there is something of a parallel. For *Missio Dei*, Liberal and Emergent *Approaches*, the distinctions between society and the local church are minimized, if not abolished, so that the lines of distinction are blurred deliberately. However, for Evangelistic and Lausanne churches, the world around them is seen as a mission field that a church must enter to serve, transform and win. In both cases, barriers and social distinctions are removed for the purpose of mission. Timmis and Chester contrast the atmosphere of the betting shop and the church, describing how the one is alien to those who frequent the other, and suggesting that both need to be familiar with the other's space.[195] Hospitality, and families extending to include their neighbours, is suggested as a missional key.

Mention has been made of the work of ministers as pastors of their communities, particularly in Welsh-medium Liberal churches. Their involvement in their communities, similar to that of a parish priest, has led to significant influence, and some additions to churches as a result. Such community-inclusive approaches have also built links into local schools and youth clubs, and with families, so that parents reconnect with the church as they move to the village and start to raise a family. Opportunities, especially in stable Welsh language communities, still exist for traditional patterns of community connection.

Compassion as a Bait or an Instinct

For Evangelistic *Approaches*, there remains a desire to rescue people from a sinful world, and incorporate them into the local church. The local church engages with its community in order to effect this rescue. Such a mission, of community engagement and service, could be perceived as having an ulterior motive, a hidden agenda different from the one initially presented. Using social action as a bait to draw people towards Christian profession may not be obvious when initial needs are being met. When

195 Timmis and Chester, *Gospel-Centred*, 24-25

Evangelistic mission is seen in this light, it implies a measure of subterfuge and deception. Mission *Approaches*, other than Evangelistic, do social action for altruistic reasons, albeit with a hope that those benefiting will consider the Christian message as a consequence. Boucher speaks of those who "love them until they ask why".[196] Social action is, in these *Approaches*, not merely a means to an end.

The impression that compassion is being used as bait, however, could be merely a matter of emphasis. The recipient of a service, be it *foodbank* or shelter, would soon suspect insincerity if the service was simply a cover. Those involved in CAP are up-front and explicit about who they are and why they are willing to help.[197] In practice, the margins between similar *Approaches* were not distinct, and, whether the inner motivation is evangelistic or altruistic, few Christians would resist those wanting to know more. If some social action was done for cynical reasons, no trace of it was evident in the questionnaire or interview responses. Churches of all *Approaches* would see compassion to the poor and needy as part of their responsibility, whether or not they would see it as part of their mission. Most E1 churches did acts of mercy for the needy as part of their pastoral ministry, or compassionate giving, perhaps hoping for a religious response, but they did not see such activity as part of their mission, alongside or in any way replacing evangelism.

Reflections on Adjustments to Social Contexts

Priorities for mission ranged from emphasising the churches' responsibility to proclaim peace with God, to providing peace on earth. Some calibrated

---

196 D. Boucher, *Taking Our Place: Church in the Community* (Cardiff: Gweini: Facevalues, 2003), 79.
197 J. Kirkby, *Nevertheless: The Incredible Story of One Man's Mission to Change Thousands of Lives* (Bradford: CAP, 2009), 189-201.

their mission to their social context more than others, but the communal, mutual, and egalitarian traits of Welsh societies mean that a church's mission needs to be relationally connected and engaged. Churches that stood apart from their communities, except for evangelistic raids into the world to rescue, or snatch converts, were declining as Christendom faded.

Financial pressures on the Welfare State's social care provisions give increasing opportunities for what has come to be known as the voluntary or "Third Sector".[198] Partnerships with local authorities enable churches to model good news, as well as proclaim it. In so doing, churches participate in the communalism and mutuality of the Welsh social context. Social action would seem to be obligatory, not merely optional, in the mission of the churches in the twenty-first century.

---

198 Boucher, *Taking Our Place*, 22-24.

Politics:
What about Caesar?

Political allegiances in Wales were described as broadly following Balsom's regional categories. British Wales, where Welsh and British identities overlap, would tend to show support for the Liberal or Conservative parties. Post-industrial Welsh Wales would be strongly Labour, but the party's monopoly was fading due to increasing disillusion. *Y Fro Gymraeg* was the heartland of the nationalist *Plaid Cymru* / The Party of Wales, though its popularity was also growing in Welsh Wales.

Wales's political landscape has changed since the founding of new Welsh national institutions in the early part of the twentieth century, and especially since the National Assembly for Wales was established in 1998. The new governance of Wales, with accessible regional policies, is giving new opportunities to churches to be involved in their communities. Contextual mission will need to respond to these changing realities, and responses may vary from a call for a pietistic non-involvement and separation, to a full identification and partnership with political bodies.

Regional Differences in Political Involvement

Leaders of the different *Approaches* to mission were aware of the political realities in different parts of Wales, and responded to them in varying ways. For churches in *y Fro Gymraeg*, issues of nationalism, and the active promotion of the Welsh language, were the dominant political issues. Churches and their members were involved through political protest and direct action, which was potentially divisive between churches serving the two language communities. Churches in such areas, which appear to be promoting English or British political loyalties will alienate the majority of the local population.

For churches in Welsh Wales, Labourism is not the homogenous force it once was, though most Councils, and the National Assembly, are Labour-led. However, churches which support government initiatives on poverty, human trafficking, the homeless, after-school clubs or street disorder and litter, have been appreciated at all levels of government. They have also received local and national government help, including funding, for their programmes. Opportunities for partnership, as well as members standing for elected positions, have increased opportunities for mission within the political sphere.

Churches in British Wales, where cross-border loyalties are strong, will encounter hostility to nationalism and the National Assembly, and will therefore have to work closely with local, not national, government. Major political issues are of a local, not a socialist or nationalist nature. One church leader was elected as an independent County Councillor, and in controversies over care in the community he was the spokesman to the national media. In this way a clear and practical demonstration of mission through political engagement was modelled.

Political Lobbying and Protest

Churches from all *Approaches* to mission were involved in lobbying and protest, and encouraged their members to participate in such action. Involvement was on an individual basis, and, apart from two churches that were openly supportive of *Plaid Cymru*, churches were decidedly apolitical in terms of support for a particular party. Political involvement was described as "small p", relating to "issues" and not party politics. This included letters or visits to members of the local Council, National Assembly or Westminster Parliament, demonstration and protest, and signing petitions. Such actions were on issues such as human trafficking, homelessness, refugees, justice, poverty, world peace, marriage legislation, and the Welsh language. For Menna Machreth, the opportunity to use the language was a matter of human rights, freedom and justice, akin to other civil rights issues that needed to be fought for. She spoke of the need for direct action by Christians through protest, and how this was needed as an end in itself, and not just a means to evangelism:

> "We can't just ignore who we are. We can't ignore the issues that have hurt us. Christians have wisdom from God and are well equipped to deal with such an inflammable issue as identity. On the other hand it's disappointing when evangelical Christians see the language as just a means to reach people for conversion rather than an essential part of their identity in Christ".[199]

The gathering of public opinion has become a valued part of policy making at all levels of government, so the lobbying activities described are welcome, and opportunities for doing so in person, or via the internet, are readily available. However, churches that are in partnership with local and Assembly politicians will have built relationships that will aid their submissions. Protestations against government policies, by churches which do not engage with government agencies practically, might be less effective because they are perceived as being solely negative in tone.

---

199 Machreth, "Ethnicity," n.p.

Partnership with Local and National Government

A number of church partnerships with local and national government have been described earlier, in which funding, expertise and cooperation were made available to churches for day centres, sports facilities, an art gallery, and the care of the elderly or mentally challenged. Such partnerships take advantage of current favourable attitudes to the voluntary sector, and lend a measure of credibility and accountability to the services the churches provide. No evidence was found of unfavourable or restrictive conditions being applied to facilities and projects being funded from public funds.

Sounding Sense

"There is a greater openness within the community, greater conversations in the street and greater recognition in the Establishment and Council ... that they need us, and we don't have to apologise for our motivation for the gospel in a way that we had to ten years ago. We are lagging behind the opportunities as churches ... there are changing perceptions of what church is... People had preconceptions of what church is ... and they don't want that! Now there is a new openness. People see a church that cares ... Local authorities are more open to help, the schools are open ... but people in church are exhausted just holding life together".

Gweini, the Council for the Christian Voluntary Sector in Wales, has a policy director who also acts as the National Assembly Liaison Officer for EA Wales. Through this role, Evangelical and Lausanne churches have an official channel and voice to all levels of government in Wales. *Gweini* provide advice on Local Authority Compacts, County Voluntary Councils, Communities First legislation and advice on fund applications from government agencies. *Gweini*'s work and support reflects the increasing attempt by E2 and Lausanne churches to adjust to the changing political climate in Wales.

Reflections on Adjustments to the Political Contexts

The more limited sphere of the political context for mission in Wales, demonstrates, all the more clearly, the outworking of the different *Approaches*. Pietism, which sees Christ's kingdom as expressed among Christian people, is in sharp contrast to Liberalism's social gospel where Christ's kingdom is to be found in the world generally. In the spectrum of views, political engagement will be seen as either a compromise or a duty. However, the greatest impact in mission was among churches where words and deeds are involved together. Some of these deeds were political action. In the words of Stott:

> "Some cases of need cannot be relieved at all without political action (the harsh treatment of slaves could be ameliorated, but not slavery itself; it had to be abolished.) ... It is always good to feed the hungry; it is better to eradicate the causes of hunger. So if we truly love our neighbours, and want to serve them, our service may oblige us to take political action on their behalf".[200]

How engagement with the political context is expressed has also changed, as political structures in Wales have evolved. The National Assembly for Wales has given increasing opportunity to local churches to contribute, and be funded, within the voluntary sector. Churches that have responded to the opportunities have made significant contributions to their communities, and created opportunities for the community to come closer to the churches, and hear the churches' message. Churches that contributed solely to the political context through protest, or lobbying for policies consistent with their convictions, may have limited their influence as a result.

Activism in defence of the language or Welsh communities will be very different from what is appropriate in post-industrial areas of extreme

---

200 J. R. W. Stott, *Issues Facing Christians Today* (Basingstoke: Marshalls, 1984), 12

deprivation, or in English-speaking border towns. In urban areas, all the activities may be appropriate in adjacent wards. The political context shows the need for churches to adapt to the changing conditions around them. It also shows the need to engage with the forces that change society, rather than passively accepting them. This calls for missional churches, which get involved in society to bring political and social change, alongside or as a bridge for spiritual salvation.

Summary:

Pointers Forward

Wales has many unique contexts for mission. The distinctives are expressed differently from region to region, like a patchwork, but common characteristics have been identified. The six different *Approaches* to mission have been seen to be effective to different degrees, and their effectiveness has been seen to be, in part, a result of how they adjusted to the *Aspects* of context. Lessons have been drawn that suggest effective practice for the future, which may assist the resurgence of Welsh churches, rather than their inevitable decline.

I have attempted to demonstrate how effectively different *Approaches* to mission have adjusted to Welsh contexts, and the conclusions drawn in Section Three will be a guide and reference for mission in Wales for the coming decades. Patterns of church that are currently hindering mission need to change, in their message and in how they calibrate their mission to their context.

- The traditional patterns of Welsh Nonconformity for church and mission have become so fixed and inflexible, that they hang over the future as a hindrance and source of irrelevance. Secularism and post-Christendom realities have changed the religious landscape in Wales to the extent that churches relying on in-pull and centripetal mission are in inevitable decline. Local churches in the twenty-first century will have to shed the traditions and formalism of the nineteenth century. Churches that are relational, not formal, in their life, contemporary in their style, and centrifugal in their mission are the churches that are growing both numerically and in their influence. It is also worthy of note that more than two-thirds of 5:2 churches were Pentecostal or New Church / Charismatic in expression, whether independent or of Baptist affiliation. Expectation of the miraculous and the Spirit's present work would seem to be a key ingredient of mission.

- As a "land of villages", Wales needs churches and mission that are local, and embedded in their community. To seek to draw people into adjacent or distant communities would seem to be adopting alien patterns which are counter-cultural to Wales's sense of *cynefin*.

- The Welsh are no longer a homogeneous *ethnie*. However, in local communities, especially those with few incomers or where new arrivals live separately from the indigenous population, mission will need to respect an assumed Welshness. Mono-ethnic groups and mission may be expressed through a multi-ethnic church community, or separate churches which cooperate to reach and serve different people groups. However, churches in areas with separate ethnic communities, which operate a policy of non-differentiation will limit those attending, and those reached, to the few in the community who desire such integration. Mission must respect ethnic distinctives whilst modelling ethnic respect and cooperation.

- The same distinctions will, inevitably, operate in communities separated by language. To insist that a vulnerable language group conforms to the dominant language group will only cause alienation, and dysfunctional mission. Church community, worship and mission must go with the linguistic grain of the wider community, and not appear to threaten it.

- Communities that are communal and egalitarian in ethos will expect the churches to be a participating part of their community life. To stand apart, seeking to draw people out of the wider community into a church community, must be counter-cultural. The churches must seek to be at the heart of their communities, even if, in terms of values and beliefs, they do not fully conform. Serving other people practically and compassionately, whether as a result of, a bridge for, or a central part of the church's mission, is indispensable.

- Wales is a nation, which now has political institutions, programmes, and policies that are accessible to individuals and churches. For mission to be effective, resourced, and even legal, it must connect and cooperate with political institutions at local and Assembly level. This political context is evolving rapidly, and the Church's mission must evolve with it.

If these adjustments are made, as Chambers says, decline is not inevitable. Indeed, he says that there are hopeful prospects, where churches are seeking to be contemporary and missional.[201] But such a future is not inevitable. It will not be secured by looking back to better

---

201 Chambers, "Out of Taste," 95-96.

days, but by giving much more attention to the future. We must understand the trends in Wales that are determining the contemporary context. The report, commissioned by the Church Missionary Society, researching the gap between churches and the culture in south Wales, speaks of a strategy of rebirth, not survival. For this the churches must be less concerned with preserving the past, and instead focus on sowing seeds into the soil of Wales today, expecting a better future.[202]

An essential element of such change is to calibrate the mission appropriately to the particular locality and context. The nature of mission must not be merely a copy from another situation or era where a particular approach was deemed effective. This is particularly true with new churches or church plants, which do not have the benefit of long-standing loyalties or connections in the community. Mission has to be 'tailor-made':

> "It is geared to need, spiritual and practical, rather than to a model that works somewhere and therefore has to work where we are... There are not many manuals on how to reach areas like the Welsh Valleys. It has to be ourselves taking the temperature and, before God, assessing how we can meet those needs case-by-case... It is being empathetic to what's going on around you."

Responding to the particularities of a locality in Wales, and adopting an appropriate mission approach, will be essential if churches in Wales are to flourish again. Our mission, in word and deed, will involve change from previous patterns, and flexibility as local contexts in Wales continue to evolve. Wales may never again be a Nonconformist nation, mono-lingual or mono-ethnic, but it will continue to value local identity and community, and may become increasingly nationalistic, Welsh-speaking and distinct from its English neighbour.

---

202 R. J. Sudworth, *The Outside-In Church: Researching opportunities for CMS in the Welsh Context* (London: Church Missionary Society, 2003), 7.

Local churches will prosper in such new opportunities if they calibrate their mission to their particular context and live out their message credibly. Jesus Christ, we believe, came into this world, walked where the people walked, and sacrificed himself to reconcile, redeem and restore. He then rose again to build his church and reign forever. Churches in twenty-first century Wales will need to proclaim the truth of what he achieved, identify with those he came for, and serve in order to see all the possible benefits secured.

Postscript

Books don't change anything unless they are read and prompt a different way of thinking and doing. Thank you for reading this far, but action must now follow. Leaders must talk to leaders, in their own church and with others, to work through how to respond. Change is always difficult, but it is easier and possible if we do it together.

Just think....

- If we all renew our commitment to the gospel of Jesus Christ and our determination to make it known. People today have little idea of their need of reconciliation with a holy God, of forgiveness through Jesus' death, and new life and hope through his resurrection.

- If we take seriously the need for outward facing, relevant and contemporary churches, with a Christian community in all local communities, people and language groups. People need to see an expression of church that they can access, relate to, and feel comfortable in.

- If we start building bridges to our communities, society and political centres, and begin to be seen as good news as well as speaking about it. People today need to see changed lives and communities if they are to consider the possibility of change for themselves.

- If we look out to adjacent communities and areas, and even farther afield, where there is no living expression of church and mission. People in these areas will not hear or see the good news unless we go to tell them.

What if we don't?

Appendix:

The Charts of the *Waleswide / Cymrugyfan* Survey

All bar charts except Chart 29

are scaled 0-100%

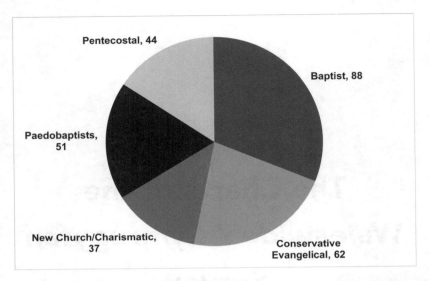

Chart 1. The proportions and numbers of leaders from different denominations completing the 2012 Survey

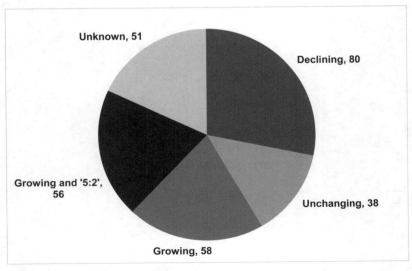

Chart 2. The Proportions and numbers of Churches Declining, Unchanged, Growing, or Growing '5:2'

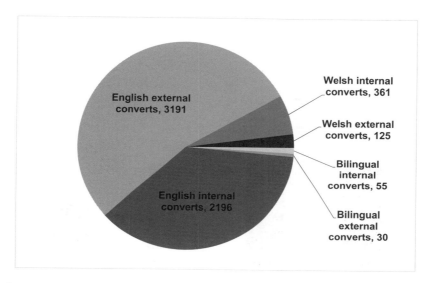

Chart 3. The proportion and number of additions from within and without the churches, according to the languages used.

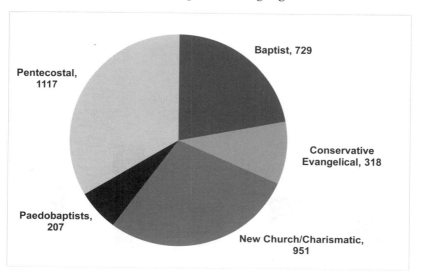

Chart 4. The proportions and number of additions in relation to denominational connection.

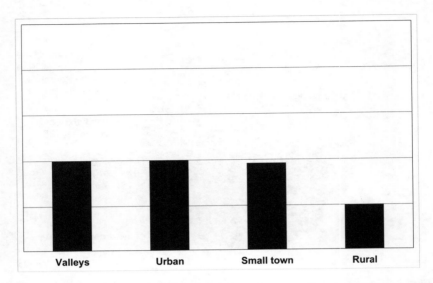

Chart 5. The proportion of all churches responding as 5:2, according to location.

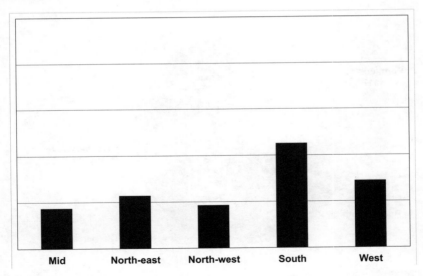

Chart 6. The proportion of churches responding as 5:2, according to area.

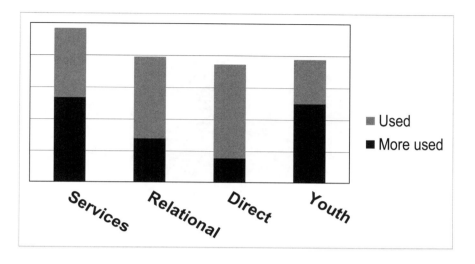

Chart 7. The proportion of churches using one or more elements of each group of methods for communicating their message.

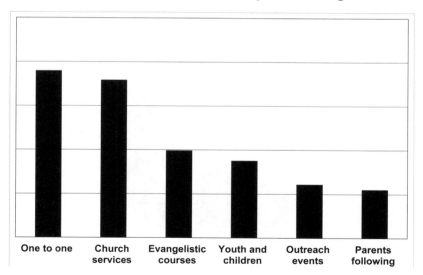

Chart 8. The methods used when individuals came to faith in Christ.

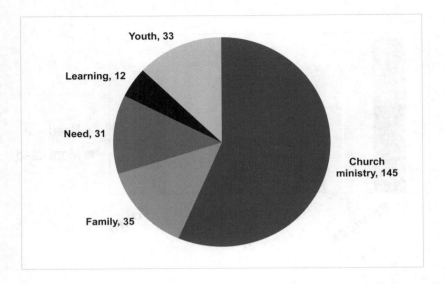

Chart 9. How the churches were connecting to their community.

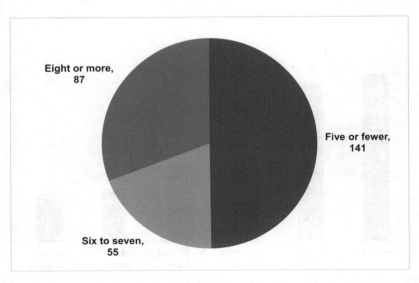

Chart 10. The number of the churches' connections to their community.

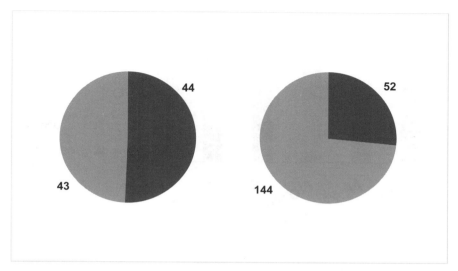

Chart 11. Churches that have 8 or more connections [left] and fewer than 8 connections [right] showing the proportion and number that are 5:2 [dark area]

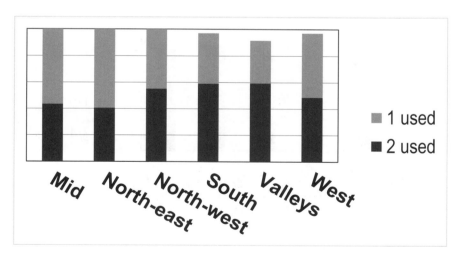

Chart 12. The % of churches using one or more activities in the Services category to promote their message, in the various regions.

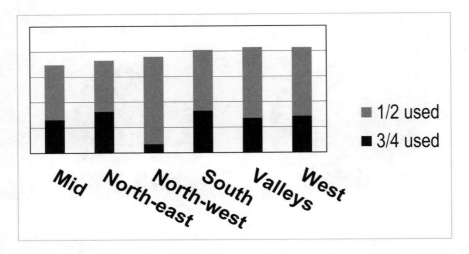

Chart 13. The % of churches using one or more activities in the Relational category to promote their message, in the various regions.

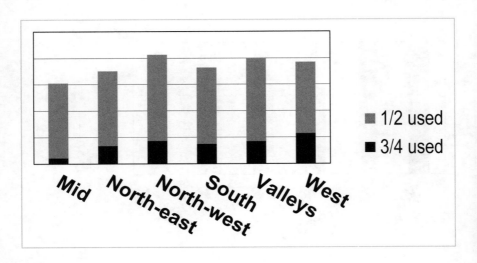

Chart 14. The % of churches using one or more activity in the Direct category to promote their message, in the various regions.

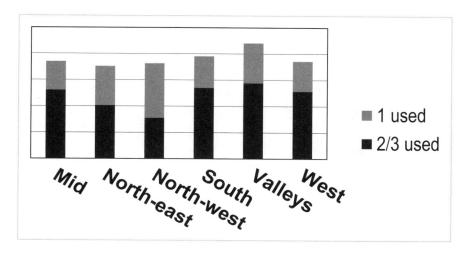

Chart 15. The % of churches using one or more activity in the Youth category to promote their message, in the various regions.

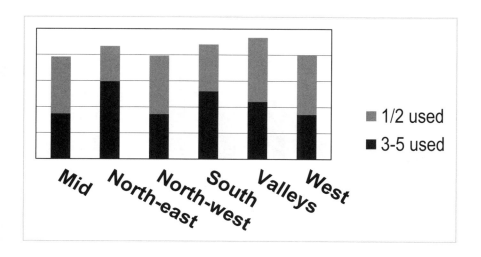

Chart 16. The % of churches using one or more Church Related activities to connect to their communities, in the various regions.

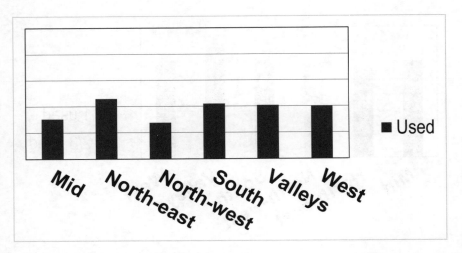

Chart 17. The % of churches using Café Related activities to connect to their communities, in the various regions.

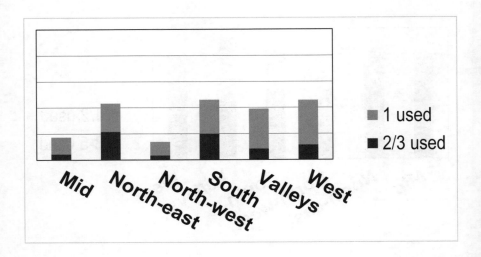

Chart 18. The % of churches using one or more Family Related activities to connect to their communities, in the various regions.

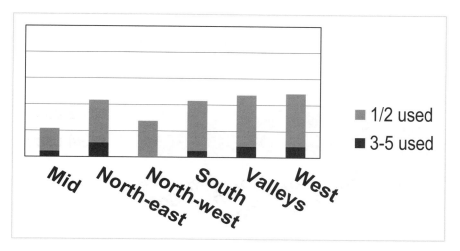

Chart 19. The % of churches using one or more Need Related activities to connect to their communities, in the various regions.

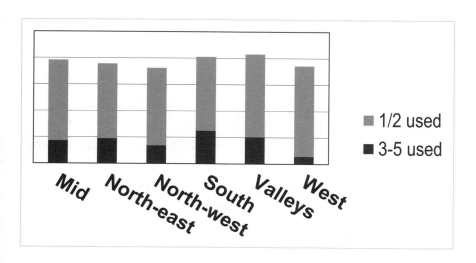

Chart 20. The % of churches using one or more Youth Related activities to connect to their communities, in the various regions.

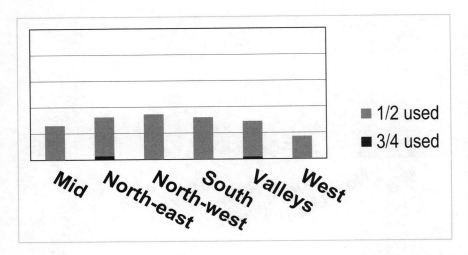

Chart 21. The % of churches using one or more Learning Related activities to connect to their communities, in the various regions.

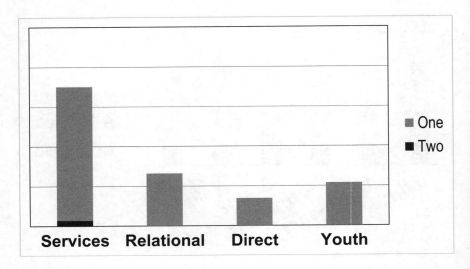

Chart 22. The evangelism methods, and how many from each category were "most used" by E1 churches.

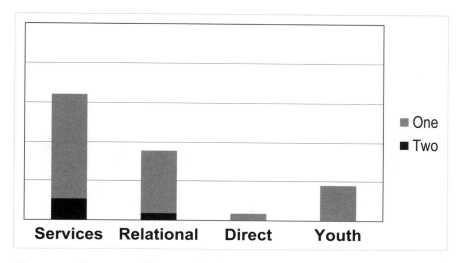

Chart 23. The evangelism methods, and how many from each category were "most used" by E2 churches.

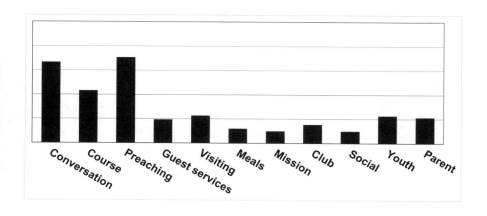

Chart 24. The percentage of E1 churches that saw people came to faith in Christ through the various means.

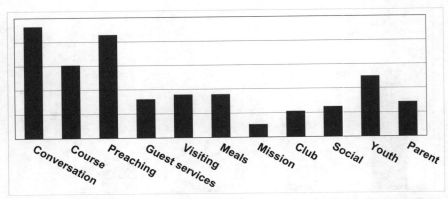

Chart 25. The percentage of E2 churches that saw people came to faith in Christ through the various means.

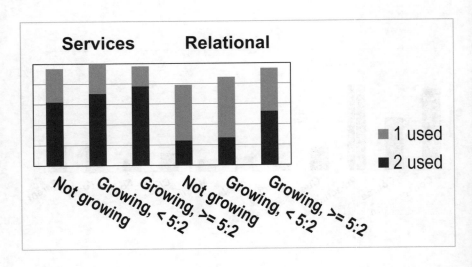

Chart 26. Evangelistic churches use of Services and Relational methods in relation to growth patterns.

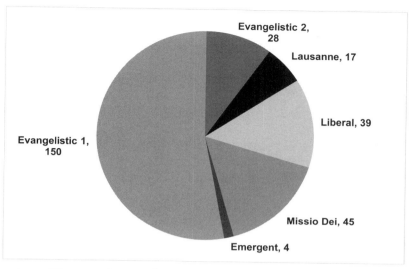

Chart 27. The number and proportion of all churches according to Approaches to mission.

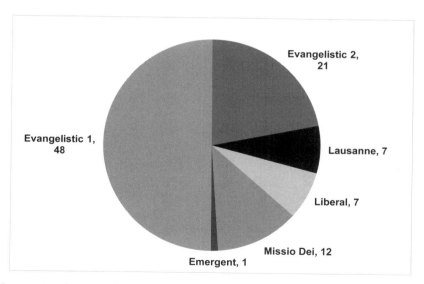

Chart 28. The number and proportion of 5:2 churches according to Approaches to mission.

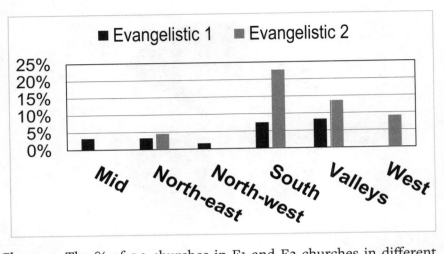

Chart 29. The % of 5:2 churches in E1 and E2 churches in different regions

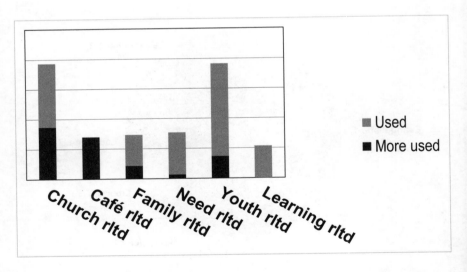

Chart 30. The degree and nature of E1 connections to community

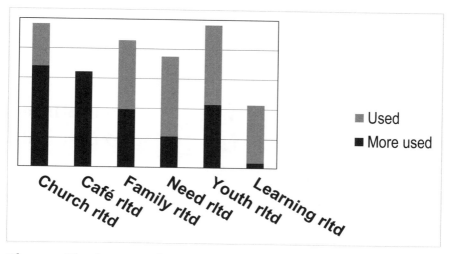

Chart 31. The degree and nature of E2 connections to community

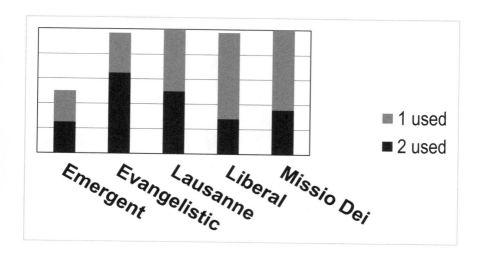

Chart 32. The % of churches using the Services methods to promote their message.

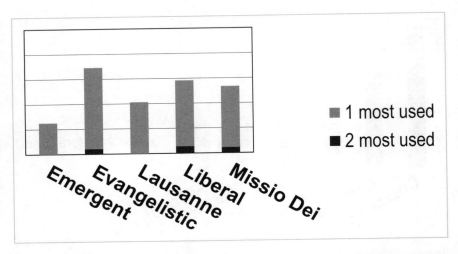

Chart 33. The % of churches using the Services methods as "most used" to promote their message.

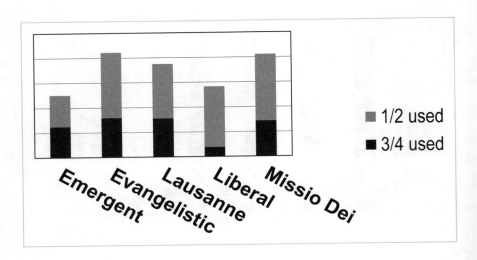

Chart 34. The % of churches using the Relational methods to promote their message.

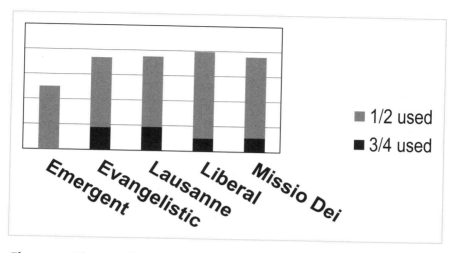

Chart 35. The % of churches using the Direct methods to promote their message.

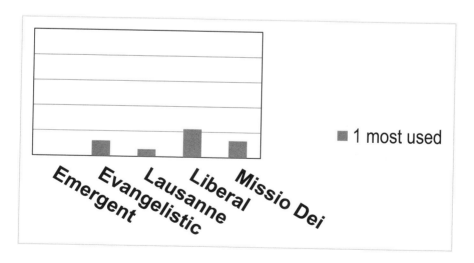

Chart 36. The % of churches using the Direct methods as "most used" to promote their message.

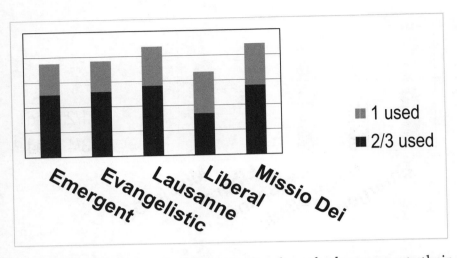

Chart 37. The % of churches using the Youth methods to promote their message.

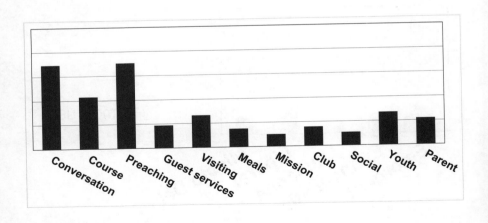

Chart 38. How people came to faith, and were added to the church, in all churches.

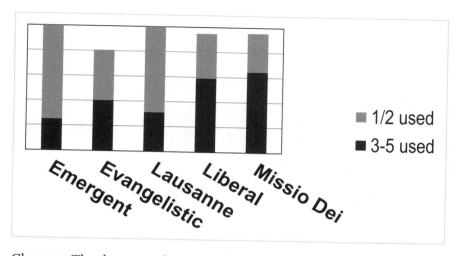

Chart 39. The degree and extent of Church Related to connect to their communities.

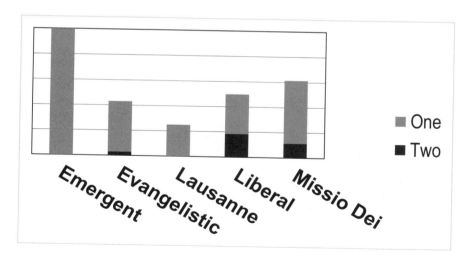

Chart 40. The degree and extent of Church Related as "most used" to connect to their communities.

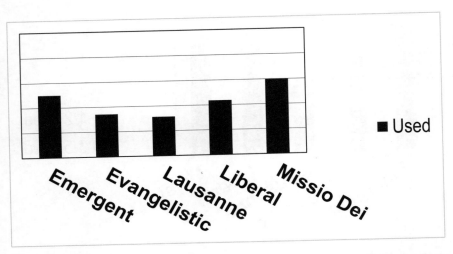

Chart 41. The degree and extent of Café Related to connect to their communities.

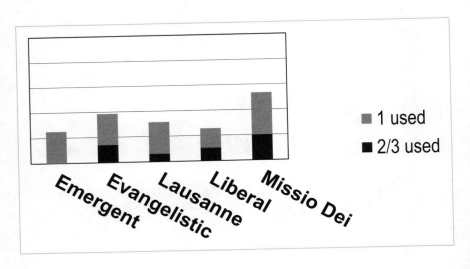

Chart 42. The degree and extent of Family Related to connect to their communities.

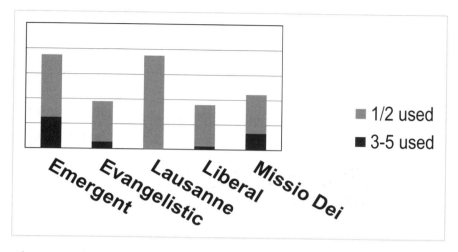

Chart 43. The degree and extent of Need Related to connect to their communities.

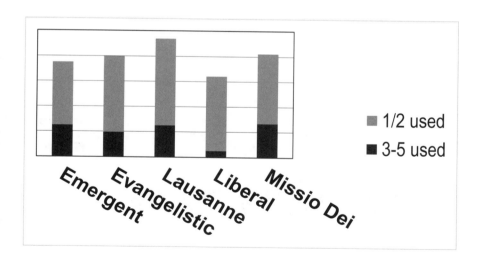

Chart 44. The degree and extent of Youth Related to connect to their communities.

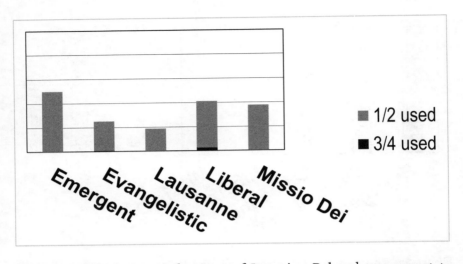

Chart 45. The degree and extent of Learning Related to connect to their communities.

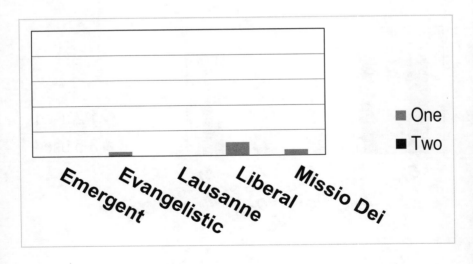

Chart 46. The degree and extent of Learning Related as "most used" to connect to their communities.

	Evangelistic	Lausanne	Missio Dei	Liberal	Emergent
Not involved	34%	0%	0%	15%	0%
National	14%	0%	25%	30%	17%
Local	34%	100%	75%	55%	67%
Lobbying	45%	50%	62%	45%	50%
Lobbying	45%	50%	62%	45%	50%

Chart 47. The Percentage of Churches Involved in Politics for each Approach to Mission

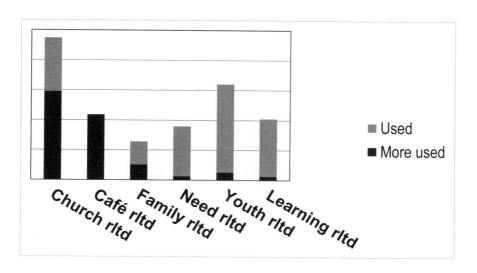

Chart 48. How Liberal churches connected to their communities, and used several approaches in a group.

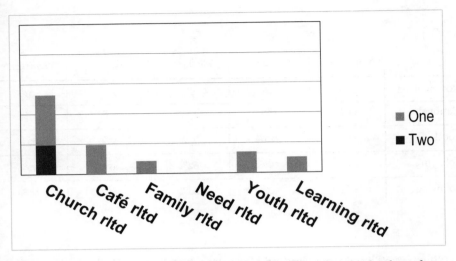

Chart 49. How Liberal churches connected most, and whether these "most used" came from the same group.

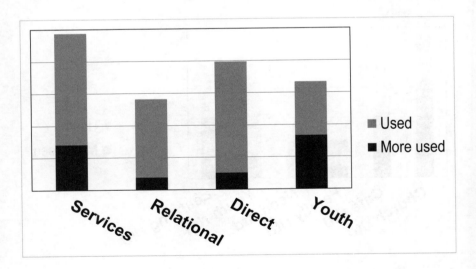

Chart 50. How Liberal churches sought to communicate their message, showing the % use of each group, and multiple approaches in a group.

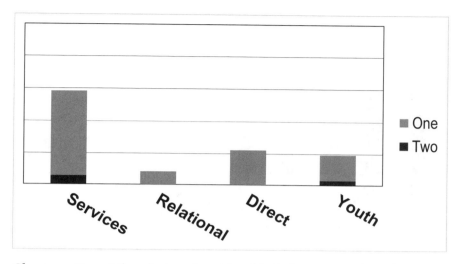

Chart 51. How Liberal churches identified the approaches they used most, and whether these "most used" came from the same group.

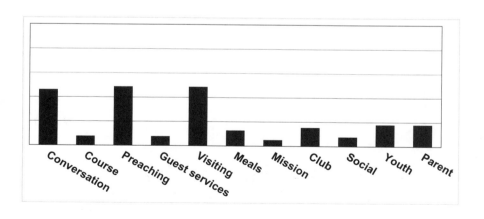

Chart 52. How people came to faith, and were added to the church, in Liberal churches.

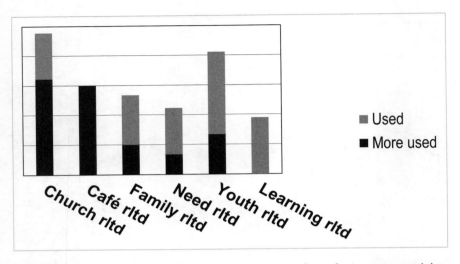

Chart 53. How Missio Dei churches connected to their communities, and used several approaches in a group.

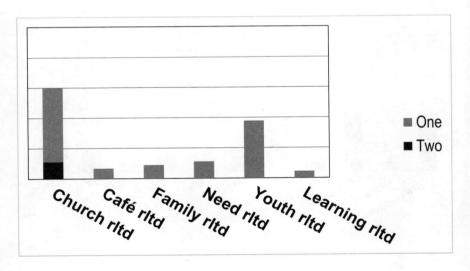

Chart 54. How *Missio Dei* churches connected most, and whether these "most used" came from the same group.

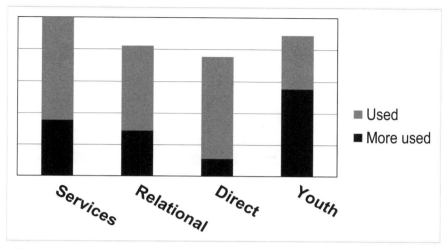

Chart 55. How *Missio Dei* churches sought to communicate their message, showing the % use of each group, and multiple approaches in a group.

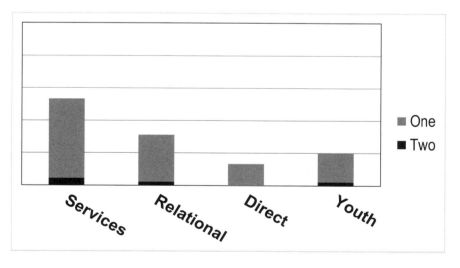

Chart 56. How *Missio Dei* churches identified the approaches they used most, and whether these "most used" come from the same group.

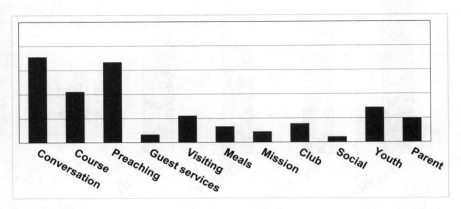

Chart 57. How people came to faith, and were added to the church, in *Missio Dei* churches.

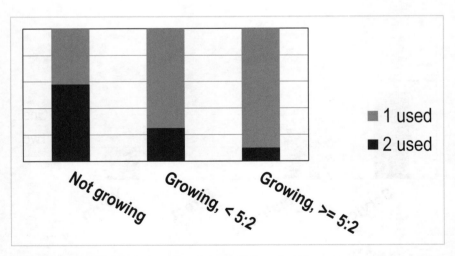

Chart 58. *Missio Dei* churches' use of Services to communicate their message, in relation to growth patterns.

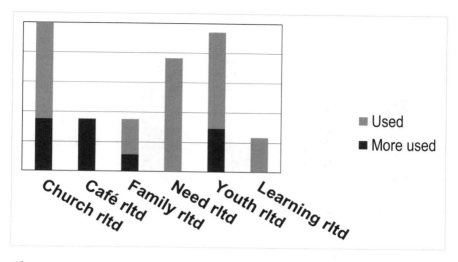

Chart 59. How Lausanne churches connected to their communities, and used several approaches in a group.

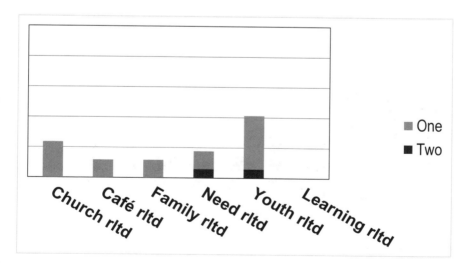

Chart 60. How Lausanne churches connected most, and whether these "most used" came from the same group.

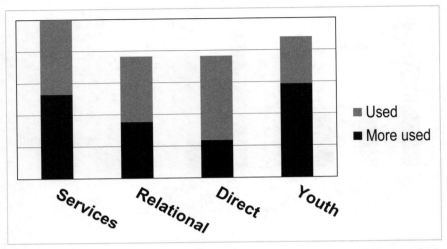

Chart 61. How Lausanne churches sought to communicate their message, showing the % use of each group, and multiple approaches in a group.

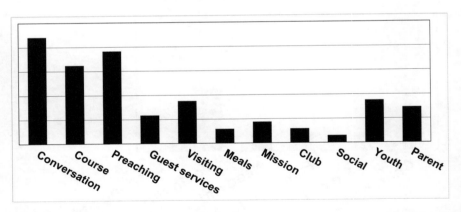

Chart 62. How people came to faith, and were added to the church, in Lausanne churches.

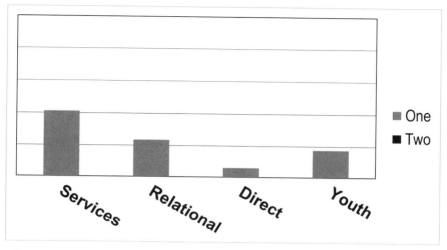

Chart 63. How Lausanne churches identified the approaches they used most, and whether these "most used" come from the same group.

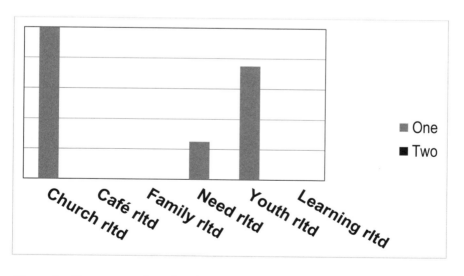

Chart 64. Emergent churches "most used" connections to community.

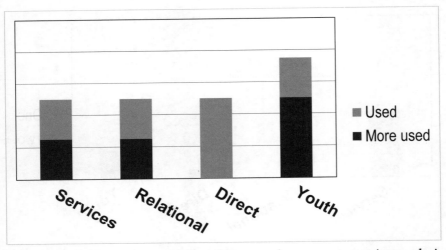

Chart 65. How Emergent churches sought to communicate their message, showing the % use of each group, and multiple approaches in a group.

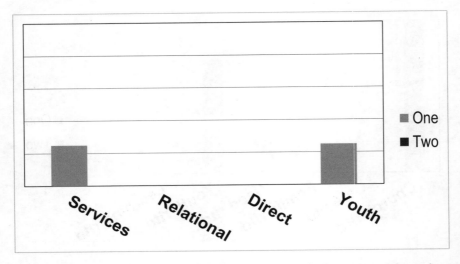

Chart 66. How Emergent churches identified the approaches they used most, and whether these "most used" came from the same group.

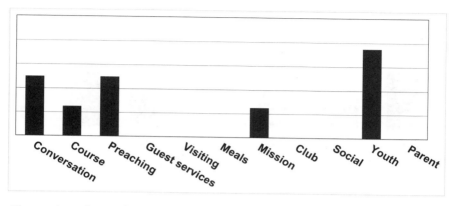

Chart 67. Through what means people were added to Emergent churches.

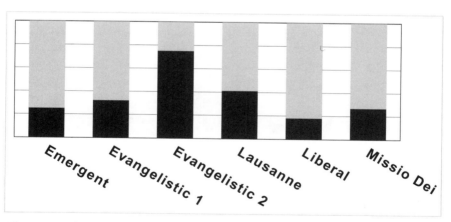

Chart 68. The proportion of 5:2 churches in each Approach to mission. (The dark shade being 5:2)

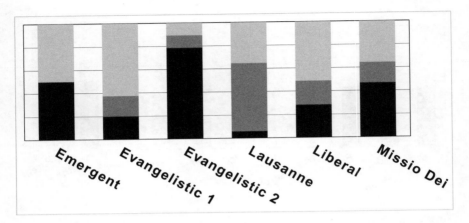

Chart 69. The proportion of churches with >5 and >7 connections to their community. (The darkest shade being >7, the mid- shade >5, and the light shade <5.